The rose is white, not re[d],
because white is the ideal co[lor]

This rose is fixed in a sky-colored background,
to show that such joy of faith
in the spirit is but a promise and
beginning of heavenly joy to come.

Around this background is a ring,
to show that such bliss in heaven is endless.

And since the ring is made of gold, the best
and most precious metal, it also shows
that the bliss of heaven is more precious
than all other joys and treasures.

Why I Am a Lutheran

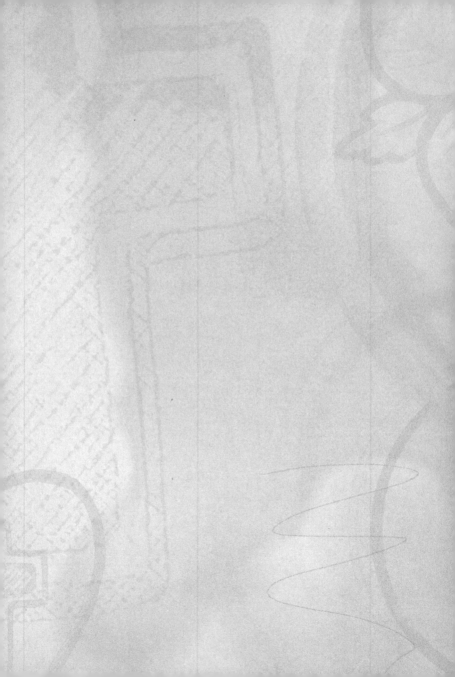

Why
I Am a Lutheran

Jesus at the Center

D a n i e l   P r e u s

CONCORDIA PUBLISHING HOUSE · SAINT LOUIS

Manufactured in the United States of America

Library of Congress Cataloging-in-Publication Data

Preus, Daniel, 1949-
    Why I am a Lutheran : Jesus at the center / Daniel Preus.
        p. cm.
Includes bibliographical references.
    ISBN 0-7586-0514-5
    1. Lutheran Church. I. Title.
    BX8065.3.P74 2004
    284.1—dc22

                                                    2003027242

2 3 4 5 6 7 8 9 10   13 12 11 10 09 08 07 06

Dedicated to two God-fearing women whose love for God's Word has been a great source of encouragement to me— my wife, Linda, and my mother, Donna.

CONTENTS

———∽∽∽———

Preface	9
Introduction: Jesus at the Center	11
1. I Am Jesus' Little Lamb	17
2. A Matter of Mountains	25
3. We Are Alive	77
4. Mount Zion and the Cross	89
5. Mount Zion and the Sacraments	107
6. Font, Pulpit, and Altar	145
7. We Will Live Forever	153
8. The Office of the Holy Ministry	165
9. Zion Sings	179
Conclusion: Lord, in Your Mercy—Hear Our Prayer	193
Appendix: Luther's Small Catechism	201
Notes	222

PREFACE

⟨≈≈⟩

Many books have been written with the intention of providing a thorough exposition of the Christian faith and the teachings of the Lutheran Church. This is not one of them. Rather, it is my hope, within the pages of one modest volume, to demonstrate what is always and only at the center of all Christian teaching—Jesus Christ and Him crucified. Apart from the birth, life, suffering, death, and resurrection of Jesus, Christianity is neither unique nor particularly helpful to sinners living under the Law of a righteous and powerful God. But in Him, in His person and work, God is revealed to us in a way that truly is unique among all world religions. Through Jesus we come to see God as gracious. He loves us; He saves us; He forgives us; He helps us constantly; He adopts us as His children and bequeaths to us an everlasting kingdom—all for the sake of Jesus. To express this life-changing message, I have attempted, as much as is possible, to limit myself to demonstrating one simple, yet profound truth: Jesus is at the center of all that is truly Christian. If I have succeeded in accomplishing this task, I will also have succeeded in answering the question: *Why am I a Lutheran?*

For the reader who wishes a concise, biblical, and ageless explanation of the basic truths of Christianity, Martin Luther's Small Catechism is attached as an appendix and should answer, at least briefly, questions I have not addressed.

I am grateful to Fritz Baue for "getting me going," Mark Sell for getting me to "knuckle down" and "flesh out," Dawn Weinstock for assistance in "fine tuning," and especially to my wife, Linda, for her patient and supportive role as a "sounding board."

I wish to express deep appreciation to the thousands of pastors who minister daily to the needs of God's people by bringing them His Word and to the countless laypeople who receive God's Word with joy and who live out their lives giving witness to the Word of truth the Holy Spirit has placed in their hearts. Above all, I thank my heavenly Father for the privilege of proclaiming His precious Gospel to those who read this book. I pray that He will use it to bless my single objective: to show people Jesus. He is the only hope for a lost and sinful world.

Daniel Preus, November 10, 2003

INTRODUCTION

JESUS AT THE CENTER

And the Word became flesh and dwelt among us, and we have seen His glory, glory as of the only Son from the Father, full of grace and truth. (John 1:14)

"I am the Alpha and the Omega," says the Lord God, "who is and who was and who is to come, the Almighty." (Revelation 1:8)

In the words of St. John's Gospel and in the Book of Revelation, Jesus identifies Himself as the only true God, who came to earth to save His people. In John 1:14, Jesus says He "tabernacles" with us (the Greek word for "dwell" is the verb form of the noun that means "tent"). He is the God who dwells on earth in the human tent called flesh. In Revelation,

Jesus refers to Himself in the same words God says to Isaiah to describe Himself (Isaiah 41:4). Therefore, Jesus is the eternal one who always has been and always will be. With these words, Jesus proclaims that the entire revelation of God given to us in the Holy Scriptures was given so we might know Him.

Jesus uses the first and last letters of the Greek alphabet (*alpha* and *omega*) to describe Himself. Thus Jesus announces that from Genesis to Revelation, from the first letter of Scripture to the last, God's Word witnesses to Him. When Jesus says to those who seek to kill Him, "You search the Scriptures because you think that in them you have eternal life; and it is they that bear witness about Me" (John 5:39), He meant more than that the Old Testament contains one or two passages that refer to Him. Rather, Jesus was stating that the Old Testament is all about Him. When the apostle John records in his Gospel that these things "are written so that you may believe that Jesus is the Christ, the Son of God, and that by believing you may have life in His name" (John 20:31), his words apply not only to his Gospel but also to all of Holy Scripture. The Bible also talks about creation, sin, Israel's history, Jesus' miracles, and much more of value for Christians, but in the final

The Scriptures were written so sinful people might come to know their Savior.

analysis, the Scriptures were written so sinful people might come to know their Savior. The simple truth that the Scriptures reveal Jesus Christ, the Savior, requires emphasis, especially when pluralism (the acceptance of all points of view as being true, even if they contradict one another) calls into question the idea, even the possibility, of truth and, therefore, the relevance of any religion that claims to reveal truth. We also live in a time when vast multitudes no longer know what Christianity is. Because we live in a nation that has provided freedom for the preaching of the Gospel, we are tempted by any number of media preachers to view the Christian faith as a set of rules to shape good behavior that pleases God. And if Christianity is defined as something little different than other world religions, it is not surprising that people forsake it in vast numbers, especially in the United States.

In one sense, a major theme of the Bible and of Christianity is our conduct as human beings. But this does not mean that we are able to please God with our behavior. On the contrary, everything we learn in the Bible about our behavior reveals that we never will and never can measure up to the requirements of God's Law. Every one of us falls short. As St. Paul says: "All have sinned and fall short of the glory of God" (Romans 3:23). So it was before a single page of the Bible was written; so it is still today. Every one of us breaks God's Law and deserves His anger. King David writes: "God looks down from heaven on the children of man to see if there are any who understand, who seek after God. They have all fallen away . . . there is none who does good, not even one" (Psalm 53:2–3).

In response to this tragic message of our inability to please Him, God reveals to us His love in the person of His Son. This message is the beating heart of Christianity. All the teachings of the Bible revolve around Jesus, its pulsating center, the Savior of the world. Because all of us are sinful and break God's commands each day, we deserve nothing but God's punishment for what we think, say, and do. But Christianity teaches that God loved the people of this world so much that He did not wish to punish us for our sinful thoughts, words, and acts. Instead, God the Father sent His Son to do what sinful people could not do. God the Son became a human being, was born of the Virgin Mary, and lived His entire life on earth so He could save sinful people and restore them to their heavenly Father. As our substitute, Jesus kept the Law perfectly for us, yet He was punished for the sins of the world, taking all our guilt on Himself and dying the death we deserved for the wrongs we had done. Because of Jesus' life, death, and resurrection, God forgives us and promises the gift of eternal life in heaven to everyone who believes in His Son.

This profound message of salvation in Christ is the Good News that all of Scripture brings to us. Centuries ago, Johann Gerhard, a Lutheran pastor and theologian, wrote that every word of the Bible is to be read as if it were printed with ink that is the very blood of Jesus. God caused every single word of the Scriptures to be written with this objective in mind: to show us His Son, our Savior. By showing us Jesus, God brings us to faith in Him, and with faith comes life.

This book, therefore, is first and foremost a book about Jesus. He is the heart, the epicenter, of the Christian faith and the only hope for sinful people, for us. We sing about this hope in the words of Martin Luther's beautiful Christmas hymn:

> "From heav'n above to earth I come
> To bear good news to ev'ry home;
> Glad tidings of great joy I bring,
> Whereof I now will say and sing:
>
> "To you this night is born a child
> Of Mary, chosen virgin mild;
> This little child, of lowly birth,
> Shall be the joy of all the earth.
>
> "This is the Christ, our God and Lord,
> Who in all need shall aid afford;
> He will Himself your Savior be
> From all your sins to set you free."[1]

CHAPTER ONE

I AM JESUS' LITTLE LAMB

One of the first hymns I remember learning as a child was "I Am Jesus' Little Lamb." Its references to pleasant pastures and quiet waters, sheep and shepherds, sparked my young imagination. What a welcome pastime for a young boy sitting in a small church as the northern Minnesota winter cast its chill over the countryside. Even as the verses of this hymn extol a shepherd's care for his flock, they proclaim a far greater love and care, namely, the love and care Jesus, the Savior, has for each of us. Even as a child, I understood that Jesus' love was completely different than the love I experienced from my family and friends. The hymn connects Jesus' love with His identity. As my Good Shepherd, Jesus guides me, provides for me, loves me, and calls me. Because of all He has done for me through His perfect life and death, I can be happy as His little lamb. And as the hymn concludes, when my life ends, "He shall fold me to his breast, There within his arms to rest."[1]

What a tremendous message. People today are involved in an exhausting search for some form of spirituality; they seek a God they cannot find. But in "I Am Jesus' Little Lamb," we sing that Jesus, our Good Shepherd, has found us. He is the God who cares for us on earth, in His Word, and in His church as we live out our lives as Christians. People need to be loved, and this hymn reminds us that Jesus does, indeed, love us and care for us. The finest love comes from Jesus and His sacrifice for us on the cross. His mission on earth was for us as He died for the sins of the entire world, including your sins and mine. Jesus paid for every last sin when He hung on the cross. That is why Jesus is our Good Shepherd.

The mission of the church is to proclaim this beautiful message throughout the world. The message begins with the Word and Sacraments in our congregations. Then the message of Jesus' love and what He has done for us moves into our family life as we love one another as moms and dads, sons and daughters, and in whatever other vocation God has given to us. Ultimately, Jesus' love and the beautiful message of the Savior go out into the community, into the world, through your pastor and the family of God.

How did the comforting message of Jesus and His work of salvation come to you? To all of us, it came through God's holy Word as we learned that Jesus is the God who became a man for our salvation. But some say the Bible isn't clear or isn't clearly the Word of God. Some say the Bible contains only the thoughts of particular men who reflected on what God might be like. This is not what the prophets and apostles testify to in the Scriptures.

THE QUESTION OF OUR AGE

"Did God actually say?" (Genesis 3:1). With this question, Satan tempted Adam and Eve to doubt the Word of God and to question its truth. After all, if God, who is the creator of all things, and His Word can be suspect, where can truth of any kind be found? Adam and Eve succumbed to Satan's temptation. Since the fall, the human race has been skeptical, always wondering, always doubting, constantly questioning the possibility of religious truth. It is our sinful nature. Distorted by sin, the quizzical and investigative propensities given to us by God have turned on their Giver and Creator.

Consider the times in which we live. Our age ridicules the notion of truth. The idea that particular statements are absolutely correct and others false has never been more unpopular. Pontius Pilate's cynical question, "What is truth?" (John 18:38) seems to be the motto of our age. Most people say, "You have your beliefs; I have mine. You have your truth; I

Our age ridicules the notion of truth.

have mine. Let's leave each other alone, and we'll both be happy." We live in a time of mass immigration, migration, and exchange of information. In addition to the fracturing of "traditional" values and definitions of right and wrong, this confluence of cultures, races, peoples, and ideas has brought unbelievable blessings and opportunities to share Christ with our neighbors.

It's ironic that in this day, when absolute truth is almost universally denied, people still yearn for it. However, because they believe that truth is unattainable, they suffer through discontented, unfulfilled, and disquieted lives, wishing for a firm place to stand against the chaos. We all become confused and bewildered as we are bombarded by friends, associates, businesses, institutions, and organizations with messages that confuse, infuriate, and frighten. We live in a time of uncertainty, unsure of so many things. Many of us lack direction as we travel through life without a compass, without a guiding star. We listen to the mixed messages of family members and friends, politicians and civic leaders, businesspeople and educators. Even preachers and theologians can't determine who is right and who is wrong. We grow cynical and more wary of those who claim to peddle "truth."

God, however, is no cynic. He is no cosmic chess player. God has provided for the removal of any uncertainty we might have concerning our relationship with Him, our salvation, and all things spiritual. God sent His Son—the truth in human flesh—to bring us the truth (John 14:6). What the

Scriptures tell us about Jesus Christ and what Jesus Christ Himself tells us in the Scriptures is true (John 17:17). We can depend on it. We can stake our lives and souls on it. Jesus says: "If you abide in My word, you are truly My disciples, and you will know the truth, and the truth will set you free" (John 8:31–32). Concerning the message that he, as one of Jesus' disciples, preached to the church, Peter writes: "We did not follow cleverly devised myths when we made known to you the power and coming of our Lord Jesus Christ, but we were eyewitnesses of His majesty" (2 Peter 1:16). Peter emphasizes this point only four verses later: "No prophecy of Scripture comes from someone's own interpretation. For no prophecy was ever produced by the will of man, but men spoke from God as they were carried along by the Holy Spirit" (2 Peter 1:20–21).

God's Word satisfies our longing and need for truth.

And in the matter of our relationship to God and our eternal salvation, we cannot afford to live in uncertainty. As a parish pastor and in my travels, I've often asked people if they believe they will go to heaven. More times than I can count I have heard the reply, "I don't know. I hope so." My heart sinks every time I hear that answer. It's absurd to think we tolerate such uncertainty regarding life's most important question. Would we act this way in any other area of our lives? For example, if someone asked if your spouse were coming home from a business trip, would you answer, "I don't know. I hope so"? Or if someone asked if you were going to be paid this month, would you answer, "I don't know. I hope so"? Or if someone asked if your child were coming home on the bus, would you answer, "I don't know. I hope so"? Even sadder than such a response to questions such as these is to offer the same "hope so" answer to the question of whether God loves you or whether Jesus saves you. How far this uncertainty is from the faith of the apostles! St. Paul says, "I am sure that neither death nor life, nor angels nor rulers, nor things present nor things to come, nor powers, nor height nor depth, nor anything else in all creation, will be able to separate us from the love of God in Christ Jesus our Lord" (Romans 8:38–39).

We do not need to live in uncertainty regarding what is true about God and our faith in Him. God does not give us truth simply so we can be correct in what we believe. God does not give us truth so we can know that we are right and those who disagree with us are wrong. God does not give us truth so we can "win the argument." Jesus, the Son of God, did not take on human flesh, did not become one of us, simply so we can know what is true. John tells us in his Gospel that when Jesus came into the world, He was full of truth and grace (John 1:14). Jesus brings truth for the sake of grace, that is, for the sake of God's undeserved kindness.

Knowing Jesus is the Son of God is essential. But unless we know and believe that Jesus is the Son of God who has come to forgive, all is for nothing. It is essential that we know and believe that Jesus died on a cross, but His death will not help us one whit unless we know that Jesus died on a cross for our sins, that His death earned our forgiveness so we can live forever with Him and all who are His. It is essential that we know Jesus rose from the dead, but it is more important that we know He rose from the dead for us so we, too, will rise one day to inherit an eternal kingdom.

Truth without grace won't help us. Moses brought truth. Moses brought the Law, and every word of it was true. But it only showed people their sins, their weaknesses, their failings, their lack of love for the God who gave that Law. It doesn't show us anything different. God's Law says: "Don't kill. Don't commit adultery. Don't lust. Don't covet. Don't disobey your parents. Don't swear. Don't use God's name in ways you should never use it. Don't neglect to worship Him, pray to Him, praise Him, and glorify Him at every opportunity." But not one of us can tolerate even a passing glance in the mirror of God's Law, much less a sustained stare. Imagine that your deepest, darkest sins were made evident some Sunday morning before the entire congregation. You'd run away because of the terror, because of the shame. God's Law strips us bare like that. God's Law, when it's taken seriously, shames and embarrasses us; it makes us turn away in fear. It shows us for what

> *The true grace Jesus brings covers every sin.*

we are—sinners. And everything we see in God's Law that embarrasses us, shames us, and frightens us is true.

But truth does not necessarily help us. We need truth that comes with grace, which is the kind of truth Jesus the Savior brings. The true grace Jesus brings covers every sin. What sins have you committed? What shameful deeds lie in your past? What hateful and harmful thoughts have you tried to ignore? What guilt haunts you in the dark dead of night? God forgives them all. He washes you clean. As John the Baptist cried, "Behold, the Lamb of God who takes away the sin of the world!" (John 1:29).

This message of truth with grace, this message of Jesus the Savior, lies at the center of Scripture, at the very heart of the Christian faith. It also is the heart of the confession of the Lutheran Church. Jesus is the Alpha and the Omega, the beginning and the end, the Good Shepherd who searches for the lost sheep and leads His flocks to pleasant pastures and quiet waters. All of Scripture and the entire Christian faith are brought into focus only when it is all about Jesus—Jesus, the incarnate Son of God, who came to bring grace that gives life to all who believe in Him.

CHAPTER TWO

A MATTER OF MOUNTAINS

---

*What does God see
when He looks at us?*

An understanding of how Jesus is at the center of Scripture and Christianity revolves around understanding why He came to earth, why He took on human flesh, why He was born of the Virgin Mary, why He suffered under Pontius Pilate, and why He died on a cross.

Jesus came to make us right with God, which means He came to *justify* us before God. The word *justify* does not frequently find itself in the vocabulary of Americans, even Christians. However, this word wonderfully describes the reason the Son of God became a man. The Greek word we translate as "justify" means "to put into a right relationship (with God), to acquit, to declare and treat as righteous, to show or prove to be right." To say that Jesus came to justify us is to say that the goal of His life and work was that we might stand before God as righteous, acquitted of all sin and guilt. To stand justified before God means that He looks on us as innocent, as pure in His eyes. But we are sinful. We have broken God's commandments. We are guilty. How can God acquit us? How can a just God justify guilty people? How can a good God declare bad people to be good?

Recall a time as a young child when you did something wrong—I mean really bad. Your father or mother probably became angry. Do you remember how you felt? You probably were afraid, anxious, and sad. After all, your parents, who were your entire world, were angry with you. Now recall a time as a young child when you did something good, something that caused your parents to brag about you. Do you remember how you felt? You probably were excited, content, happy. These examples get at the heart of what it means to be justified. God looks at us and, on the basis of what He sees, declares us to be just or unjust. If God declares us unjust, then, of course, He is unhappy with or angry at what He sees. If God declares us just, then that means He is happy with what He sees.

If God is angry with us, we are afraid because He is the all-powerful God who created all things. At His word everything came into being, and if one who is so powerful becomes angry, surely the results will be terrible. In fact, Scripture includes examples of what happens when God becomes angry. Because of their sin, God sent a flood to wipe out all human beings from the world; He saved only eight people—Noah and his family (Genesis 6–8). Because of their sin, the cities of Sodom and Gomorrah and their inhabitants were destroyed by fire from the sky, though God spared Lot and his daughters (Genesis 19). Even based on only these two accounts, if God is angry with me, I am going to be afraid. On the other hand, if God is pleased with me, if God is happy with what He sees when He looks at me, I am going to be happy. As Paul writes: "If God is for us, who can be against us?" (Romans 8:31). This God is not only the God who judges and punishes sin but also the God who has prepared an eternal kingdom of glory and joy for all those on whom His favor rests.

Is God angry with you and me? He is if He sees sinful people, lawbreakers, commandment violators. Is God happy, pleased, and delighted with you and me? He is if He sees just, righteous, innocent, holy, and pure people. What does God see when He looks at us? To answer this crucial question, we can look at three biblical mountains: Mount Sinai, Mount Calvary, and Mount Zion. All three mountains help answer the question of what God sees when He looks at you and me. All three mountains explain why Jesus is at the center of Scripture and the Christian faith.

MOUNT SINAI

When my oldest son was 9 months old, he was attracted to live plants. He didn't just like to look at them, he liked to grab them, shake them, and throw around the dirt. There-fore, he had only one parental commandment: Do not touch the plants.

At this time in my son's life, I was serving as a vicar (an internship for future pastors) in Havre, Montana. One Sun-day, I gave a children's sermon on the topic of original sin and the truth of David's confession in Psalm 51:5: "and in sin did my mother conceive me." On this particular Sunday, I had asked my wife to bring my son forward to sit with the rest of the children. As part of the children's sermon, I shared with the children and the congregation my son's fas-cination with plants and our edict to him concerning touch-ing plants. I also had brought along a plant as a visual aid, which, of course, I inadvertently placed right in front of my son. Now he knew the law, but my son looked at me, he looked at his mother, he looked at the plant, he looked at the congregation, he looked at me again—and he grabbed the plant! Yes, as every congregation knows, even pastor's kids are infected with sin. Like Adam, my son had only one com-mandment, but he couldn't keep it.

On Mount Sinai, God gave Moses the Ten Command-ments. The writer to the Hebrews tells us that whoever comes to this mountain cannot touch it because it is

> a blazing fire and darkness and gloom and a tem-pest and the sound of a trumpet and a voice whose words made the hearers beg that no further mes-sages be spoken to them. For they could not endure

> the order that was given, "If even a beast touches the
> mountain, it shall be stoned." Indeed, so terrifying
> was the sight that Moses said, "I tremble with fear."
> (Hebrews 12:18–21)

The writer of Hebrews does not exaggerate about this
mountain and the penalties incurred by those who touch it.
We read in the Book of Exodus about God's instructions to
Moses regarding Mount Sinai: "And you shall set limits for
the people all around, saying, 'Take care not to go up into the
mountain or touch the edge of it. Whoever touches the
mountain shall be put to death'" (Exodus 19:12). Three days
after these instructions were given, Moses records that God
came down on the mountain and

> there were thunders and lightnings and a thick cloud
> on the mountain and a very loud trumpet blast, so
> that all the people in the camp trembled. . . . Mount
> Sinai was wrapped in smoke because the LORD had
> descended on it in fire. The smoke of it went up like
> the smoke of a kiln, and the whole mountain trem-
> bled greatly. And as the sound of the trumpet grew
> louder and louder, Moses spoke, and God answered
> him in thunder. (Exodus 19:16, 18–19)

If you had been there with the children of Israel and
had seen, heard, and felt these things, how would you have
reacted? The Bible tells us: "Now when all the people saw the
thunder and the flashes of lightning and the sound of the
trumpet and the mountain smoking, the people were afraid

and trembled, and they stood far off and said to Moses, 'You speak to us, and we will listen; but do not let God speak to us, lest we die' " (Exodus 20:18–19). This is what happens when sinful people are confronted by God's holy Law. This is what happens when God's commandments peel away the thin, false veneer of human righteousness to reveal the guilt and shame that lie beneath. It is as if a storm takes place within the human soul and we see what we are, what we have done, our failures, our faults, our sins—and we are afraid.

Before Adam and Eve sinned, God's Law caused them no fear. They had been created in God's image, holy and pure. But after Adam and Eve disobeyed God, they were afraid. They hid as God walked in the garden. God had to call out to Adam, who answered, "I heard the sound of You in the garden, and I was afraid" (Genesis 3:10). Adam knew that God would confront him with his sin against God's command: "But of the tree of the knowledge of good and evil you shall not eat, for in the day that you eat of it you shall surely die" (Genesis 2:17). Adam and Eve had every reason to be afraid.

It has been the same for all human beings since that time. Cain killed his brother Abel and, when God confronted him with this murder, Cain was afraid (Genesis 4). Joseph's brothers sold him into slavery, and many years later, when facing discovery, they were afraid (Genesis 45:3). When David considered his sin of adultery with Bathsheba, he was afraid. In one psalm, David describes how he felt when he would not confess his wrong: "When I kept silent, my bones wasted away through my groaning all day long. For day and night Your hand was heavy upon me; my strength was dried up as by the heat of summer" (Psalm 32:3–4). David was afraid and cried out: "Hide Your face from my sins" (Psalm 51:9). When Jonah was thrown into the sea and swallowed by a great fish, he reflected on his rebellion that caused him to flee from God and defy God's will. Jonah knew that God had every right to be angry with him, but from the belly of the fish, he cried out to the Lord for mercy (Jonah 2).

―――∞∞∞―――

God's Law produces fear when people break it, but people do not want to be afraid.

To exorcize this fear, our postmodern society has done everything possible to dilute God's Law. Society does its best to abbreviate, adumbrate, and eliminate God's Law. We live in an age in which people no longer wish to believe in laws that bind them because if they did, they would be guilty and afraid when they broke those laws. Thus almost every sin that God forbids—especially those actions that debauch the sanctity of the family—is justified today by those who wish to commit it. Abortion is justified in the name of love and individual choice. Homosexual behavior is justified in the name of acceptance. Adultery and fornication are justified in the name of freedom.

Not only sins against other people have been rationalized but also sins against God. Many people consider themselves fine Christians yet never darken the door of a church building. The name of God and the name of Jesus have become exclamations to strengthen a point, with no thought of the God whose name is being abused. The First Commandment has been abandoned, even by a large portion of the so-called Christian community. A growing majority undoubtedly would take the view that it would be intolerant and bigoted to say that only Christians worship the true God. In today's society, all gods are the same and all religions have an equal claim on the truth. Thus the First Commandment—"You shall have no other gods before Me" (Exodus 20:3)—has become irrelevant, and if the First Commandment is irrelevant, so is the Holy Trinity. If the Holy Trinity is irrelevant, then so is the Lord's Prayer. All that remains is a generic god who, at best, maintains order but cannot save anyone. If this generic god is accepted in the church, then the Christian faith is no longer focused on Jesus. At best we can say that people are striving for some sort of spirituality, but there seems to be no substance to that spirituality.

Society has done all it can to eliminate God's Law and thereby extinguish God's anger. If God's anger has been extinguished, then all penalty for sin, all punishment, also is eradicated. Thus the message of Sinai is silenced. The thunder can no longer be heard. The lightning cannot be seen.

The quaking cannot be felt. The smoke cannot be smelled nor does it irritate the eyes. Because we do not wish to be afraid, we have abolished everything that could frighten us. We have become the center and purpose of our own lives, and we believe that we justify ourselves. We may create God in our own image so we can justify ourselves to whatever weak and anemic god we create. Or we don't bother with a god at all. And if we do away with God's Law, with His anger at sin, with Him, then we don't have to worry about justification and righteousness at all.

In the face of such rebellion and defiance, Jesus says: "Truly, I say to you, until heaven and earth pass away, not an iota, not a dot, will pass from the Law until all is accomplished" (Matthew 5:18). To those who do away with the second table of God's Law (the Fourth through the Tenth Commandments, which are about love for our neighbor), St. Paul says: "Do you not know that the unrighteous will not inherit the kingdom of God? Do not be deceived: neither the sexually immoral, nor idolaters, nor adulterers, nor men who practice homosexuality, nor thieves, nor the greedy, nor drunkards, nor revilers, nor swindlers will inherit the kingdom of God" (1 Corinthians 6:9–10). Paul makes essentially the same point to the church in Ephesus (Ephesians 5:3–6) and to the church in Galatia:

> The works of the flesh are evident: sexual immorality, impurity, sensuality, idolatry, sorcery, enmity, strife, jealousy, fits of anger, rivalries, dissensions,

divisions, envy, drunkenness, orgies, and things like these. I warn you, as I warned you before, that those who do such things will not inherit the kingdom of God. (Galatians 5:18–21)

To those who would do away with the first table of God's Law (the First through Third Commandments, which are about love for God), and particularly the First Commandment, God says: "How should My name be profaned? My glory I will not give to another" (Isaiah 48:11). In Exodus 34:14, God says: "You shall worship no other god, for the LORD, whose name is Jealous, is a jealous God." In the words of the Third Commandment, God declares: "You shall not take the name of the LORD your God in vain, for the LORD will not hold him guiltless who takes His name in vain" (Exodus 20:7). To clarify the First Commandment, our Lord Jesus says: "I am the way, the truth, and the life. No man comes to the Father except through Me" (John 14:6). The apostle John also testifies: "No one who denies the Son has the Father" (1 John 2:23). In other words, what God did on Mount Sinai still stands. The Law God gave on Mount Sinai still stands. We may stop our ears so we cannot hear it, but the thunder still rumbles. We may close our eyes, put on a blindfold, or even put out our eyes, but the lightning still flashes. And the Word still goes out: "Whoever touches the mountain shall be put to death." (Exodus 19:12).

> *No one who denies the Son has the Father.*

All of us have touched this mountain. The Book of Genesis describes us when it records that "the LORD saw that the wickedness of man was great in the earth, and that every intent of the thoughts of his heart was only evil continually" (Genesis 6:5). There are no exceptions to King Solomon's statement that "there is no one who does not sin" (1 Kings 8:46) or to Paul's statement that "all have sinned and fall short of the glory of God" (Romans 3:23). Thus in the Augsburg Confession, which is part of our Lutheran Confessions, we read:

> Our churches also teach that since the fall of Adam all men who are propagated according to nature are born in sin. That is to say, they are without fear of God, are without trust in God, and are concupiscent [desire evil]. And this disease or vice of origin is truly sin, which even now damns and brings eternal death on those who are not born again through Baptism and the Holy Spirit.

> Our churches condemn the Pelagians and others who deny that the vice of origin is sin and who obscure the glory of Christ's merit and benefits by contending that man can be justified before God by his own strength and reason.[1]

King David says: "Behold, I was brought forth in iniquity, and in sin did my mother conceive me" (Psalm 51:5). Our lives testify repeatedly that what David confessed is true. We are sinful from birth. We call this teaching original sin.

From the time of Adam and Eve, all people have been born sinful and are in rebellion against God unless brought to faith by the power of the Holy Spirit through the Gospel.

In the Book of Leviticus, God says to us, "You shall be holy, for I the LORD your God am holy" (Leviticus 19:2). This is the message of Mount Sinai. If we come to meet God on this mountain, we do so knowing this mountain is holy and anything unholy that touches this mountain will die (Exodus 19:12). Standing on Sinai, we will never appear before our God as holy, pure, and just. We have laid our hands on God's Law and we have broken it. We touch Sinai every day. There is no justification for the sinner on this mountain. There is only lightning and thunder, God's anger and death.

But there is one who can stand on this mountain. That person is God in the flesh, Jesus Christ. Jesus is the new Adam who can touch Mount Sinai and not burn or die. He is the one who fulfilled God's holy Law for us. However, the guilt and the death that result from our sin must be addressed, which our Lord provides for too. The same Jesus traveled from Mount Sinai to another mountain to take care of the consequences of sin for us.

MOUNT CALVARY

Despite what we are, despite what we have done, God loves us. Our heavenly Father knows we can't meet Him on Sinai, so He sent Jesus, His Son, there for us. Now God points us to another mountain, a mountain on which we can meet Him and live. In Isaiah 25, God comforts His people as He describes this mountain: "And [on this mountain] He will swallow up death forever; and the LORD God will wipe away tears from all faces, and the reproach of His people He will take away from all the earth, for the LORD has spoken" (Isaiah 25:8). God says through Isaiah that He will remove "the reproach of His people" on this second mountain. This will be a completely different kind of mountain, one where sins and tears are washed away. It will be a mountain of forgiveness and triumph over death. It will be a mountain where Jesus endures the wrath of God and pays for sin by suffering eternal death for us. The name of this mountain is Calvary.[2] The Son of God had been walking toward this mountain His entire earthly life.

In the Garden of Gethsemane, Jesus prays in anguish: "My Father, if it be possible, let this cup pass from Me; nevertheless, not as I will, but as You will" (Matthew 26:39). Jesus does not look forward with eagerness to what is coming at Mount Calvary—far from it. Yet when the time comes, Jesus meets His trials, suffering, and death with resolve. After His prayer, Jesus finds His disciples sleeping and says, "See, the hour is at hand, and the Son of Man is betrayed into the hands of sinners. Rise, let us be going; see, my betrayer is at hand" (Matthew 26:45–46). Thus Jesus marches toward Calvary, the mountain where He will endure the wrath of God and die, the mountain where He will finish everything He came to accomplish.

Upon Mount Calvary, we can meet our God without fear because the Son of God gave up His life on this mountain to wash away all our sins, guilt, and shame. With sin, guilt, and shame gone, we now can stand before God, righteous and pure. He is not angry when He looks at us because He sees holy and sinless sons and daughters. God looks at us and declares us to be just because of what Jesus has done. This is the meaning of Mount Calvary.

But how can we be justified and declared innocent because of what Jesus has done? To answer this question, we must explore a central, indeed fundamental, Christian concept. This concept is so important in both the Old and the New Testament that those who don't understand it are unable to understand Jesus or who He is. It's the concept of substitution.

In simple terms, a substitute takes the place of another. Everything the substitute does has the same value as if the original person does it. Consider, for example, that you are a starter for the Lutheran Lions, who are playing basketball against the Pagan Penguins. Within the first 30 seconds of the game, you foul out and the coach puts in a substitute. The substitute plays a stellar game, and the Lutheran Lions win. The substitute's points are counted just as if you had scored them. You don't go home and tell your family the other team won because you fouled out. No, you announce, "We won! I fouled out in the first 30 seconds, but we won!" Imagine, however, that the coach of the Pagan Penguins approached your coach after the game to inform him that the Penguins had won because the points scored by your substitute didn't count because he was only a substitute. But that isn't how the game is played. Everybody knows that whatever the substitute does is as valid as if the original person does it.

Jesus was our substitute in every way.

God gave us rules by which we were supposed to live, but we broke those rules. We fouled out of the game of life, so to speak, right at the start. From conception we have rebelled against God's rules, and we have been breaking them ever since. Because of how we have lived, there could be no victory at the end of the game. We were headed for a certain loss. Then God sent in a substitute. He sent His own Son to take our place and do what we were unable to do. We should have kept the Law, but we didn't. Instead, our substitute kept God's Law for us.

The night on which He was betrayed, Jesus prayed to His Father: "I have glorified You on earth, having accomplished the work that You gave Me to do" (John 17:4). The work the Father had given Jesus was that of keeping the Law on our behalf. The writer to the Hebrews tells us that Jesus did everything without sin (Hebrews 4:15). We were supposed to love God with all of our heart and soul and mind. We didn't, but our substitute did so for us. Jesus says in the Gospel of John: "I have kept My Father's commandments and abide in His love" (John 15:10).

We were supposed to be punished for our sins, for breaking God's rules and commandments, but God sent a substitute for that too. Jesus was punished in our place, bearing our sin and guilt so we could go free. John the Baptist says succinctly: "Behold, the Lamb of God, who takes away the sin of the world!" (John 1:29). Isaiah says it beautifully:

> Surely He has borne our griefs and carried our sorrows; yet we esteemed Him stricken, smitten by God, and afflicted. But He was wounded for our transgressions; He was crushed for our iniquities; upon Him was the chastisement that brought us peace, and with His stripes we are healed. All we like sheep have gone astray; we have turned every one to his own way; and the LORD has laid on Him the iniquity of us all. (Isaiah 53:4–6)

But Jesus did more than take on our punishment and death. He was our substitute in every way on every day of His life. Everything we should have been, our substitute was. Everything we should have done, our substitute did. Everything we should have suffered, our substitute suffered. Because Jesus kept every commandment perfectly, our God looks at us as if we had kept every commandment perfectly. Jesus took care of Mount Sinai for us, and He took care of us on Mount Calvary when He died on the cross for our sins. Therefore, God looks at us as if we already had died on the cross and paid for our sins. After all, our substitute did it for us.

Jesus was our substitute with every breath He took, with every step He walked, with every word He spoke, with everything He did. From the moment of His conception in Mary's womb to the moment of His death, Jesus took our place. Whether it was obeying His stepfather, Joseph, whether it was showing love to His mother, Mary, whether it was looking for food or for a place to sleep—everything Jesus did, He did for you and me. He wasn't on this earth for Himself. Thus when Jesus went into the desert to be tempted (Matthew 4), He did it for us. He went to be tempted as our substitute, to resist temptation on our behalf. After resisting Satan's temptations without sin, Jesus stood before God as our substitute.

Perhaps the most profound expression of substitution in the Bible is found in Paul's Epistle to the Galatians: "Christ redeemed us from the curse of the law by becoming a curse for us—for it is written, 'Cursed is everyone who is hanged on a tree'" (3:13). Luther comments extensively on this verse in his "Lectures on Galatians":

> Paul guarded his words carefully and spoke precisely. . . . For he does not say that Christ became a curse on His own account, but that He became a curse "for us." Thus the whole emphasis is on the phrase "for us." For Christ is innocent so far as His own Person is concerned; therefore He should not have been hanged from the tree. But because, according to the Law, every thief should have been hanged, therefore, according to the Law of Moses,

Christ Himself should have been hanged; for He bore the person of a sinner and a thief—and not of one but of all sinners and thieves. For we are sinners and thieves, and therefore we are worthy of death and eternal damnation. But Christ took all our sins upon Himself, and for them He died on the cross. Therefore it was appropriate for Him to become a thief and, as Isaiah says (53:12), to be "numbered among the thieves."

And all the prophets saw this, that Christ was to become the greatest thief, murderer, adulterer, robber, desecrator, blasphemer, etc., there has ever been anywhere in the world. He is not acting in His own Person now. Now He is not the Son of God, born of the Virgin. But He is a sinner, who has and bears the sin of Paul, the former blasphemer, persecutor, and assaulter; of Peter, who denied Christ; of David, who was an adulterer and a murderer, and who caused the Gentiles to blaspheme the name of the Lord (Rom. 2:24). In short, He has and bears all the sins of all men in His body—not in the sense that He has committed them but in the sense that He took these sins, committed by us, upon His own body, in order to make satisfaction for them with His own blood. . . . But just as Christ is wrapped up in our flesh and blood, so we must wrap Him and know Him to be wrapped up in our sins, our curse, our death, and everything evil. . . .

Surely these words of Paul are not without purpose: "Christ became a curse for us" and "For our sake God made Christ to be sin, who knew no sin, so that in Him we might become the righteousness of God" (2 Cor. 5:21). . . .

This is the most joyous of all doctrines and the one that contains the most comfort. It teaches that we have the indescribable and inestimable mercy and love of God. When the merciful Father saw that we were being oppressed through the Law, that we were being held under a curse, and that we could not be liberated from it by anything, He sent His Son into the world, heaped all the sins of all men upon Him, and said to Him: "Be Peter the denier; Paul the persecutor, blasphemer, and assaulter; David the adulterer; the sinner who ate the apple in Paradise; the thief on the cross. In short, be the person of all men, the one who has committed the sins of all men. And see to it that You pay and make satisfaction for them." Now the Law comes and says: "I find Him a sinner, who takes upon Himself the sins of all men. I do not see any other sins than those in Him. Therefore let Him die on the cross!" And so it attacks Him and kills Him. By this deed the whole world is purged and expiated from all sins, and thus it is set free from death and from every evil. But when sin and death have been abolished by this one man, God does not want to see anything else in the whole world, especially if it were to believe, except sheer cleansing and righteousness. And if any remnants of sin were to remain, still for the sake of Christ, the shining Sun, God would not notice them.

This is how we must magnify the doctrine of Christian righteousness in opposition to the righteousness of the Law and of works. . . . . If the sins of the entire world are on that one man, Jesus Christ, then they are not on the world. But if they are not on Him, then they are still on the world. Again, if Christ Himself is made guilty of all the sins that we have all committed, then we are absolved from all sins, not through ourselves or through our own works or merits but through Him. But if He is innocent and does not carry our sins, then we carry them and shall die and be damned in them. "But thanks be to God, who gives us the victory through our Lord Jesus Christ! Amen." (1 Cor. 15:57).[3]

Substitution is essential to the understanding of Christianity. When we understand this concept, we receive immeasurable comfort because we know that Jesus did everything necessary for our salvation. As our substitute, the Son of God not only took our place under the Law, which He kept perfectly on our behalf, but He also is the Lamb of God who bore our sin. Jesus' suffering and death on the cross is not a symbolic act in which God signifies His desire to reconcile us to Himself. Christ's work itself is the reconciliation. When Christ was punished as the bearer of the sin of the whole world, all the world was punished by God. When God poured out His wrath on Christ, He poured out His wrath on all people. When Christ died for our sins, the curse God pronounced on Adam in the Garden of Eden was executed on all humanity from the time of Adam to the Day of Judgment. Thus God's punishment on us already has been carried out on Jesus, our substitute. Now we can understand why we stand justified before our God: Christ has taken on Himself everything that could condemn us and has taken it all away. This is why St. Paul can say: "There is therefore now no condemnation for those who are in Christ Jesus" (Romans 8:1).

C. F. W. Walther, the Missouri Synod's first president, frequently depicted Jesus as our substitute in the same way Luther did. In a sermon on Mark 16:1–8, Walther preached on the theme "Christ's Resurrection—Your Absolution." In this sermon, he declared:

> Jesus, when He was raised from the dead, was absolved for all sin, but since it was not for Himself but for all people that Christ died, who was it really that was set free, who was it really that was absolved when Jesus rose from the dead? It was all people! Just as all Israel triumphed when David defeated Goliath, so all humanity triumphed when Jesus defeated sin, death and hell. And so we hear Paul saying in his second epistle to the Corinthians, "We

are convinced that one has died for all; therefore all have died." And again in his epistle to the Romans, "Then as one man's trespass led to condemnation for all men, so one man's act of righteousness leads to acquittal and life for all men." Just as Christ's condemnation was the condemnation of all mankind, Christ's death the death of all mankind, Christ's payment the payment for all mankind, even so Christ's life is now the life of all mankind, His acquittal the acquittal of all mankind, His justification the justification of all mankind, His absolution the absolution of all mankind.[4]

What a beautiful, comforting message! Not only has Christ taken on Himself all our sins and made them His own, but He has given to us His righteousness and made it ours. Luther called this the "blessed exchange" that occurs between Christ and the sinner. Because of this blessed exchange, Christ has taken our place and we take our place before God in Christ. In other words, the Father looks on His Son as if He were all sinners and the Father looks on us sinners as if we were His Son. In "The Freedom of a Christian," Luther compares Christ to a bridegroom and the church to a harlot whom Christ has made His bride.

Here this rich and divine bridegroom Christ marries this poor, wicked harlot, redeems her from all her evil, and adorns her with all his goodness. Her sins cannot now destroy her, since they are laid upon Christ and swallowed up by him. And she has that righteousness in Christ, her husband, of which she may boast as of her own and which she can confidently display alongside her sins in the face of death and hell and say, "If I have sinned, yet my Christ, in whom I believe, has not sinned, and all his is mine and all mine is his."[5]

In a sermon entitled "Two Kinds of Righteousness," Luther addresses the same theme:

Therefore a man can with confidence boast in Christ and say: "Mine are Christ's living, doing, and speaking, his suffering and dying, mine as much as if I had lived, done, spoken, suffered, and died as he did." Just as a bridegroom possesses all that is his bride's and she all that is his—for the two have all things in common because they are one flesh [Gen. 2:24]—so Christ and the church are one spirit [Eph. 5:29–32]. . . .

Through faith in Christ, therefore, Christ's righteousness becomes our righteousness and all that he has becomes ours; rather, he himself becomes ours.[6]

Clearly the righteousness of the Christian, the righteousness by which we stand justified before God, is not our own righteousness—it's an alien righteousness, a righteousness that comes not from within us but from outside of us. It is the righteousness of Jesus. Thus we sing, "Jesus, your blood and righteousness My beauty are, my glorious dress."[7]

If the righteousness of Jesus covers us, it cannot be imperfect or incomplete in any way because it is the righteousness of the Son of God. Therefore, it is a perfect and infinite righteousness. When God looks at you and me and sees this righteousness of Jesus that through faith has become ours, He actually sees perfection in us.

Mount Calvary offers this righteousness because on Calvary Jesus completes everything He has done for us. If Mount Sinai offers death to all who touch it, Mount Calvary offers life. Just as the woman who touched the hem of Jesus' garment was healed (Luke 8:43–48), so all who live because of the sacrifice of Jesus made on Calvary's cross are healed of all sin, guilt, and blame.

> Blest the children of our God,
> They are bought with Christ's own blood;
> They are ransomed from the grave,
> Life eternal they shall have:
> With them numbered may we be
> Here and in eternity!
>
> They are justified by grace,
> They enjoy the Savior's peace;
> All their sins are washed away,
> They will stand in God's great day:
> With them numbered may we be
> Here and in eternity![8]

Mount Sinai or Mount Calvary—where will we look for hope? If we look to our own goodness and works for justification before God, we go to Sinai without Jesus. There is no hope for us there. Sinai will only kill us. St. Paul says: "Now we know that whatever the law says it speaks to those who are under the law, so that every mouth may be stopped, and the whole world may be held accountable to God. For by works of the law no human being will be justified in His sight" (Romans 3:19–20). But Paul immediately tells us where we do have hope:

> But now the righteousness of God has been manifested apart from the law, although the Law and the Prophets bear witness to it—the righteousness of God, through faith in Jesus Christ for all who believe. For there is no distinction: for all have sinned and fall short of the glory of God, and are justified by His grace as a gift, through the redemption that is in Christ Jesus. (Romans 3:21–24)

One of my favorite hymns insists that in matters of salvation only Christ is to be glorified:

> Thy works, not mine, O Christ
> Speak gladness to this heart;
> They tell me all is done,
> They bid my fear depart.
> To whom save Thee, who canst alone
> For sin atone, Lord, shall I flee?[9]

The subsequent verses begin with the phrases "Thy wounds, not mine, O Christ"; "Thy cross, not mine, O Christ"; and "Thy death, not mine, O Christ." Each verse ends with the same rhetorical question: "To whom save Thee, who canst alone for sin atone, Lord, shall I flee?" Finally, the hymn concludes with the confession:

> Thy righteousness, O Christ,
> Alone can cover me;
> No righteousness avails
> Save that which is of Thee.
> To whom save Thee, who canst alone
> From sin atone, Lord, shall I flee?[10]

As sinful, human beings, we don't want to be sent to Sinai to touch it on our own. We don't want to trust our own lives or works for comfort. We don't want to look inside ourselves for God's favor. As St. Paul says: "For I know that nothing good dwells in me" (Romans 7:18). Instead, our comfort, assurance, and hope come from Jesus, who alone atones for sin and whose righteousness has merit before God.

---

*Our comfort, assurance,
and hope come from Jesus.*

We turn to Jesus because though He was without sin, He took our sin on Himself and touched Mount Sinai for us. Jesus, who became "sinner" in our place, was condemned and crucified for us. So we look to Him who loved us so much that He died for us. We see the glory of Mount Calvary as we look to Jesus, who alone is holy and just, who alone redeems, saves, and justifies. He has done everything necessary for our salvation. Apart from Jesus there is no hope, no forgiveness, no eternal life. Not only is He at the center of God's plan of salvation—Jesus *is* the plan.

MOUNT ZION

> For you have not come to what may be touched, a blazing fire and darkness and gloom and a tempest . . . . But you have come to Mount Zion and to the city of the living God, the heavenly Jerusalem, and to innumerable angels in festal gathering, and to the assembly of the firstborn who are enrolled in heaven, and to God, the judge of all, and to the spirits of the righteous made perfect, and to Jesus, the mediator of a new covenant, and to the sprinkled blood that speaks a better word than the blood of Abel. (Hebrews 12:18, 22–24)

When you and I became Christians, we came to Mount Zion, that is, we became members of the church, which is the family of God. This church is one throughout the whole world, and it is one in heaven. There are not two Zions, but one. There are not two churches, there is one. As members of the church, we enter an awesome family fellowship with thousands of angels, with archangels, and with all those family members now living in the heavenly Jerusalem who are one with the earthly Jerusalem. This fellowship is with God the Father who cares and loves His family and continues to send His Son to be with His family. This fellowship is the eternal feast of everlasting righteousness, which is given to the family of God by the Lamb who was slain. And the Lamb now feeds the Father's family with Word and Sacraments. All this we accept, know, and confess through faith in Christ. But how do we get this faith in Jesus? How do we become members of the Father's family, the church? How do we become Christians?

First, Jesus has done absolutely everything necessary for our salvation. When Jesus cried out from the cross that it was finished (John 19:30), He was declaring that nothing more needed to be done to redeem people from sin, death, and hell. God's love for the world sent Jesus to suffer and die for everyone. Nevertheless, unless we believe what the Scriptures tell us about Jesus, His life and work will be of no benefit to us. He loves the world, but does Jesus love me? C. F. W. Walther helps us understand the answer to this question.

> Now that Christ has been raised from the dead, no one needs to think to himself, "If I approach God with my sins, what will God do? Will He really forgive them?" No, whoever you are, whatever you have done, God has already forgiven your sins, forgiven them already 1900 years ago when in Christ, through His resurrection, He absolved all for whom Christ died on the cross. Have you cheated or stolen? It is a damnable sin—but you have been forgiven. Have you committed adultery? It is an offense against God—but you have been forgiven. Have you

been drunk time and time again? It is a shameful thing—but you have been forgiven. Have you intentionally ruined the reputation of another person? That is a terrible sin—but you have been forgiven. . . . Christ rose for you. His resurrection is your absolution. You have been forgiven.[11]

Immediately after this proclamation, Walther says:

One thing needs still to happen in order that you may *possess* this forgiveness which has been given to you—that one thing is faith. For every person who wants to be saved and go to heaven must believe that this absolution pronounced at Christ's resurrection 1900 years ago was also pronounced upon him. In order to be saved, it is necessary to believe that the forgiveness God offers is yours.[12]

Although Jesus has done everything necessary to save us, it is necessary for us to believe that He has done so if we are to be saved. Christians are not universalists who believe that because Jesus died for everybody, everybody goes to heaven. Jesus says: "Whoever believes and is baptized will be saved, but whoever does not believe will be condemned" (Mark 16:16). This teaching is clear throughout the Scriptures, both in the Old and the New Testaments. There is no salvation apart from faith in the true God. Jesus says: "Unless one is born again he cannot see the kingdom of God" (John 3:3). Although it is true that "in Christ God was reconciling the world to Himself, not counting their trespasses against

The Holy Spirit calls us to faith by means of the Gospel.

them" (2 Corinthians 5:19), those who do not believe this message of grace receive none of its blessings. It is through faith alone that we receive this righteousness of Christ so God looks on us as righteous and just. Both the prophet Habakkuk and the apostle Paul say that "the righteous shall live by faith" (Habakkuk 2:4; Romans 1:17). Paul also says, "By grace you have been saved through faith" (Ephesians 2:8), and the apostle John tells us that "God gave us eternal life, and this life is in His Son. Whoever has the Son [whoever believes in Jesus] has life; whoever does not have the Son of God does not have life" (1 John 5:11–12).

Thus the doctrine of justification belongs not only in the Second Article of the Apostles' Creed, in which we consider the person and work of Christ, but also in the Third Article, which talks about faith and how we are brought to faith. How are we brought into the church? How are we brought to Mount Zion, the heavenly Jerusalem? One of the classic answers of the Lutheran Church to these questions is found in Luther's explanation to the Third Article.

> I believe that I cannot by my own reason or strength believe in Jesus Christ, my Lord, or come to Him; but the Holy Spirit has called me by the Gospel, enlightened me with His gifts, sanctified and kept me in the true faith. In the same way He calls, gath-

ers, enlightens, and sanctifies the whole Christian church on earth, and keeps it with Jesus Christ in the one true faith.[13]

The Holy Spirit calls us to faith by means of the Gospel. The Gospel is the Good News about Jesus our Savior and all He has done to bring us into a right relationship with God. It is the Good News about how Jesus took care of Mount Sinai and Mount Calvary for us. It is the Good News about Jesus our substitute who lived according to the Law, our substitute who bore the punishment for our sin, our substitute who conquered death through His death, our substitute who rose from the dead so we, too, will rise to live with God forever. The Holy Spirit uses the message of the Gospel to bring us to faith, and this is the only way people are brought to faith, the only way the church is created.

What is the church? Our Lutheran Confessions describe it in Article 12 of the Smalcald Articles: "[T]thank God, a seven-year-old child knows what the church is, namely, holy believers and sheep who hear the voice of their Shepherd."[14] By definition, the church is all those who believe in Jesus, but there are other definitions of the word *church*. It can refer to a local congregation. It can refer to a building. It can designate a particular denomination. It even can be used to describe all those who belong to Christian denominations or who call themselves Christians. The statement "There are more than a billion members of the Christian church worldwide" does not mean that all these people actually trust in Christ, pray to God regularly, or believe in Him. Rather, such a statement indicates how many people go by the name *Christian*. The most common understanding of the word *church* comes from the Bible, in which it means "believers." The church is made up of those who confess their sins, look to Christ for mercy and forgiveness, and hear the voice of their Good Shepherd, Jesus. This church cannot be seen. It is of the heart (Luke 17:21; Romans 10:9–10). This unseen church exists throughout heaven and earth and exhibits particular marks or signs, which are outward identifiers in much the same way the Gateway Arch marks the city of St. Louis, the White House marks Washington, D.C., and the Golden Gate Bridge marks San Francisco.

The church is marked by the Word of God and its faithful and truthful proclamation. The church is marked by the rite of Holy Baptism and the proper practice of the Lord's Supper. We can't "see" the church throughout heaven and earth, but we can see the church's marks: the Word of God and the Sacraments. We can hear the preaching of God's Word and identify the church's faithfulness to that Word. We can see the waters of Baptism that the Word declares to be the washing and regeneration of those who are stained by sin. We can see the bread and wine and know that in, with, and under these earthly elements is the resurrected body and blood of Jesus Christ, as He tells us in His Word. These Sacraments give us the forgiveness of sins, which is the key that unlocks the doors to heaven. Where these marks are seen and heard as God gave them in His Word, we can be sure the church is alive and well. Thus the size of a congregation is not an accurate indicator of the church's presence nor of the church's spiritual health. Numbers do not indicate anything about the presence or strength of God's church. Rather, His church is present where there are believers, and there always will be believers in Jesus when God's Word is preached faithfully and His sacraments administered correctly.

The Word of God gives birth to the church.

How are believers made? How is the church created? Actually, these are the same question, which the Smalcald Articles answers: "In these matters, which concern the external, spoken Word, we must hold firmly to the conviction that God gives no one his Spirit or grace except through or with the external Word."[15] The Word of God gives birth to the church, nourishes the church, strengthens the church, preserves the church, and sustains the church to the end. The Word of God alone causes the church to grow. The prophet Isaiah records our heavenly Father's promise concerning His Word: "As the rain and the snow come down from heaven and do not return there but water the earth, making it bring forth and sprout, giving seed to the sower and bread to the eater, so shall My word be that goes out from My mouth" (Isaiah 55:10–11).

The Holy Spirit gives birth to the church and grows the church through the Word, through the proclamation of the Gospel. The Law does not create, sustain, or strengthen faith; it will only kill. Only the message about Jesus our Savior, our substitute through whom we have forgiveness and eternal life, creates and sustains faith. Through the preaching of the Scriptures or in the Sacraments, the Holy Spirit places this gracious message before sinners who are burdened with sin and guilt. The proclamation of the Law confronts sinners with their sin. Then the Gospel gives life to sinners who were "dead in the trespasses and sins" (Ephesians 2:1). By showing sinners the Savior who loved the world and gave Himself for it, the Gospel raises sinners from spiritual death to spiritual life.

God takes us to Mount Sinai so we can see our sin. God takes us to Mount Calvary to witness the consequence of sin, the wrath of God, which brings death. But the message of the Gospel is that Jesus took care of the required holiness of Mount Sinai and took care of God's wrath against sin by taking on Himself the punishment of death on Mount Calvary. God brings us and all Christians to Mount Zion only through the Gospel.

But is this message clearly heard in our era of mixed messages? We hear about spirituality and faith almost daily from political and civic leaders, from radio and television personalities. These voices would have us believe there are many different ways to come to Mount Zion. Confusing messages about spirituality, faith, and even "Jesus" confront us. Many people even believe that "Christian-sounding" cults such as the Mormons provide access to Mount Zion when in fact these groups deny the Holy Trinity, the divinity of Jesus, and many other basic teachings of Christianity.

When people are not content to find salvation only on Mount Calvary and do not want to accept what the Bible teaches about how one comes to Mount Zion, confusion is the result. People wish to return at least in part to Mount Sinai and face God's Law by themselves. When we wish to depend on something other than the grace revealed in Jesus and in His justifying work on our behalf, there will be confusion. To counteract this confusion, we need to emphasize the truth and clarity of God's love for people in Jesus. He fully understood the sinful realities of the world, and His love for this sinful world resulted in His own death. But when people reject or refuse to believe what God has revealed concerning Mount Sinai, Mount Calvary, and Mount Zion, they end up confused.

One of the most dangerous attacks against the Christian faith occurs when people or churches teach a different way to Mount Zion, which may occur when important teachings about sin, faith, and conversion are misconstrued or misunderstood. As the Book of Ecclesiastes says: "There is nothing new under the sun" (1:9), which is why we continue to confront the same old theologies that have contradicted the Gospel of Jesus in the past. In the fourth century, the church had to fight against the teachings of Pelagius, who believed that humans entered the world morally indifferent and could develop a moral germ or spark that led to salvation. In the sixteenth century, the church had to defend the truth of God's Word against Arminius, who taught that human beings cooperate in their conversion. The teachings of these two men denied original sin and were condemned by the church, but now they appear again in the twenty-first century.

The denial of original sin and the affirmation of free will contribute to the destruction of the Christian faith because they deny the biblical teaching that we are saved by grace alone, through faith alone, in Christ alone. Jesus and His work are obliterated as the focus and heart of the church when original sin is denied and free will is promoted. Instead of the Christian faith focusing on Jesus, it focuses on Jesus *and* the person, who through the exercise of free will contributes to his or her salvation.

When we deny the reality of original sin, we are saying we have the ability to please God with our lives and conduct. Such a teaching returns us to the foot of Mount Sinai—by ourselves. As we stare at the power and force of the Law without Christ, we discover that we have failed, and we despair. But if we deny original sin, the despair is even greater because we must possess the ability to obey, the power to do right and please God. Thus we not only return to Mount Sinai but also must live there and somehow

If we never come to Mount Calvary,
we can never live on Mount Zion.

achieve what Sinai demands—perfection, holiness—by ourselves. As long as we delude ourselves into believing that we can please God with our works and lives, we will never flee to Jesus and Mount Calvary, where our salvation is complete.

Denial of original sin and the affirmation that the human will is free are opposite sides of the same coin. If we are not sinful from birth, then we can exercise our will with complete freedom. Thus we can choose right from wrong and decide whether we will obey or disobey God's commandments. Furthermore, we are able to decide whether we will believe in Jesus.

God's Word does teach that we can exercise our will freely in earthly matters. For example, we are free to choose what to have for breakfast, in what profession we wish to serve, whom and when to marry, etc. On the other hand, because of the biblical teaching of original sin, we do not believe that human beings have a free will in spiritual matters. St. Paul says: "The natural person does not accept the things of the Spirit of God, for they are folly to him, and he is not able to understand them because they are spiritually discerned" (1 Corinthians 2:14). Unless the Holy Spirit working through the Gospel raises us to spiritual life, we will remain in spiritual bondage.

Most of what we hear on radio and television is American Protestantism, which reflects Arminian and Pelagian views of original sin and conversion. Once a person has such an important role to play in spiritual matters, these inaccurate theological views become prevalent and difficult to eradicate. Harold Senkbeil reflects on the effects Arminius and Pelagius have had on American Christianity:

> After the revivals of the late 1700s and the early 1800s, the free will of man in conversion was an incontrovertible truth for most American Protestant Christians. "After (Jonathan) Edward's time revivalist theology in America moved steadily toward emphasizing the human side of religious experience. This tendency was manifested in various ways of positing the free and decisive character of the human free will. Free will was virtually an American dogma; indeed it was practically an unassailable article of faith for most of western culture. It was also a concept that was a great aid to evangelism, which seemed most effective when based clearly on personal 'decision.' "[16]

The belief that one can make a personal decision to accept Jesus, to bring oneself out of unbelief and into faith, is possible only when one accepts the Arminian view that there is no original sin. If our will is free from the moment of conception onward, then what David says in Psalm 51 is untrue: "Behold, I was brought forth in iniquity, and in sin did my mother conceive me" (51:5). Untrue would be St. Paul's description of the Ephesians before their conversion to the faith: "You were dead in the trespasses and sins in which you once walked" (2:1–2). Luther also agrees with David and Paul when he describes the human will in "Bondage of the Will":

> So man's will is like a beast standing between two riders. If God rides, it wills and goes where God wills: as the Psalm says, "I am become as a beast before thee, and I am ever with thee" (Ps. 73:22–3). If Satan rides, it wills and goes where Satan wills. Nor may it choose to which rider it will run, or which it will seek; but the riders themselves fight to decide who shall have and hold it.[17]

The scriptural teachings concerning original sin and humanity's lack of free will in spiritual matters is routinely denied by many religious movements in the United States. Just consider the altar calls of various TV preachers, which include the invitation to make a decision for Jesus. But the conviction that the human will is free to choose God has been popular for hundreds of years. The preacher Walter Scott (1796–1861) spoke about the three things that one does in connection with becoming a Christian and the three things God does. According to Scott, faith consists in accepting the proposition that "Jesus is the Christ" (which Scott called "the golden oracle"). Second, if faith is genuine, repentance follows logically (almost automatically) and is motivated by

Christ's authoritative promises. Third, Baptism for the remission of sins is an obedient response to the Lord's command, making one's commitment complete. These are the three things an individual does, but God also does three things. First, God fulfills His promise by granting remission of sins, then He gives the Holy Spirit and eternal life.[18]

Many people loved the simplicity of Scott's message. It is said that for thirty years Scott "converted" a thousand people each year through his preaching. Yet look at what Scott credits to the human will: faith, repentance, and Baptism. But the Bible gives the Holy Spirit credit for the creation of faith. The Bible teaches that God works repentance in us through the power of His Word. The Bible teaches that Baptism is not a person's act of commitment toward God but God's gift of life to the needy sinner. Thus every work that Scott requires of us is a work that sinful human beings are incapable of doing. But God by His grace does these works in us, and we take no credit for the wonderful gift of salvation through Christ. God alone deserves the glory.

Charles Finney (1792–1875), another American preacher, deserves the greatest credit for the false but pervasive views of many Americans concerning original sin, free will, and the nature of conversion. Finney advocated that "each person had the responsibility to decide for himself to accept Christ or to be damned forever."[19] One of his most popular sermons was entitled "Sinners Bound to Change Their Own Hearts." Elsewhere Finney referred to original sin as "an anti-

Scriptural and nonsensical dogma."[20] Finney's commitment to the teachings of Pelagius was so strong that he left no room for the work of the Holy Spirit. Instead, human beings were entirely responsible for their own conversion. If he insisted that human beings are not sinful by birth and that they have a free will, it was not illogical for Finney to conclude that we also can please God with our conduct. Ultimately, Finney concluded that humans could become perfectly holy in this life through the strength of their own will. In fact, when Finney was asked if a Christian stopped being a Christian when he sinned, he answered:

> Whenever he sins, he must, for the time being, cease to be holy. This is self evident. Whenever he sins, he must be condemned; he must incur the penalty of the law of God . . . . If it be said that the precept is still binding upon him but that with regard to the Christian, the penalty is forever set aside, or abrogated, I reply, that to abrogate the penalty is to repeal the precept; for a precept without penalty is no law. It is only counsel or advice. The Christian, therefore, is justified no longer than he obeys, and must be condemned when he disobeys . . . . In these respects, then, the sinning Christian and the unconverted sinner are upon precisely the same ground.[21]

If Christians ultimately are responsible for their own conversion and sanctification, thus leaving out the Holy Spirit, and if the Christian is not guilty by virtue of original sin, then is there a place for Christ in Finney's theology? Unfortunately, in the theology of Charles Finney, Christ loses His place of honor. Thus Finney describes his view of Christ's substitutionary atonement in this manner:

> The doctrine of an imputed righteousness, or that Christ's obedience to the law was accounted as our obedience, is founded on a most false and nonsensical assumption. After all, Christ's righteousness could do no more than justify himself. It can never be imputed to us . . . . It was naturally impossible, then, for him to obey in our behalf. This representing of the atonement as the ground of the sinner's justification has been a sad occasion of stumbling to many.[22]

Based on this position, it is no surprise to hear Finney say, "Perseverance in obedience to the end of life is also a condition of justification."[23] Thus Finney turns Christianity on its head and confesses his faith as follows: "Present sanctification, in the sense of present full consecration to God, is another condition of justification. Some theologians have made justification a condition of sanctification, instead of making sanctification a condition of justification. But this, we shall see is an erroneous view of the subject."[24] Ultimately, Finney denies the scriptural view of Sinai, Calvary, and Zion.

Although serious in their defective anthropology, the Arminian and Pelagian views of free will and original sin are more egregious because they denigrate the Holy Spirit and His work. These heresies not only elevate the ability of human beings vastly above what they are able to do—namely, nothing—but also rob God of His glory by minimizing or even eliminating the work of the

The Holy Spirit is given to us as a gift of God's grace.

Holy Spirit in the act of conversion. The Holy Spirit does not come to us in response to an act of our will. He is given to us as a gift of God's grace. We do not grasp the Holy Spirit. God gives us the Spirit. The following passages from Holy Scripture emphasize this fact.

> But, as it is written, "What no eye has seen, nor ear heard, nor the heart of man imagined, what God has prepared for those who love him"—these things God has *revealed* it to us through the Spirit. The Spirit searches everything, even the depths of God. For who knows a person's thoughts except the spirit of that person, which is in him? So also no one comprehends the thoughts of God except the Spirit of God. Now we have *received* not the spirit of the world, but the Spirit who is from God, that we might understand the things freely *given* us by God. And we impart this in words not taught by human wisdom but taught by the Spirit, interpreting spiritual truths to those who are spiritual. The natural

person does not accept the things of the Spirit of God, for they are folly to him, and he is not able to understand them because they are spiritually discerned. (1 Corinthians 2:9–14, *emphasis added*)

Therefore I want you to understand that no one speaking in the Spirit of God ever says "Jesus be accursed!" and no one can say "Jesus is Lord" except in the Holy Spirit. (1 Corinthians 12:3)

It is God who . . . has anointed us, and who has also *put* His seal on us and *given* us His Spirit in our hearts as a guarantee. (2 Corinthians 1:22, *emphasis added*)

He who has prepared us for this very thing is God, who has *given* us the Spirit as a guarantee. (2 Corinthians 5:5, *emphasis added*)

Because you are sons, God has *sent* the Spirit of His Son into our hearts, crying, "*Abba!* Father!" (Galatians 4:6, *emphasis added*)

And you were dead in the trespasses and sins in which you once walked, following the course of this world, following the prince of the power of the air, the spirit that is now at work in the sons of disobedience—among whom we all once lived in the passions of our flesh, carrying out the desires of the body and the mind, and were by nature children of wrath, like the rest of mankind. But God, being rich in mercy, because of the great love with which He loved us, even when we were dead in our trespasses, *made us alive* together with Christ—by grace you have been saved—and raised us up with Him and seated us with Him in the heavenly places in Christ Jesus, so that in the coming ages He might show the immeasurable riches of His grace in kindness toward us in Christ Jesus. For by grace you have been saved through faith. And this is not your own doing; it is the *gift* of God, not a result of works, so that no one may boast. For we are His workmanship, *created* in Christ Jesus for good works, which God prepared beforehand, that we should walk in them. Therefore remember that at one time you Gentiles in the flesh, called "the uncircumcision" by what is called the circumcision, which is made in the flesh by hands—remember that you were at that time separated from Christ, alienated from the commonwealth of Israel and strangers to the covenants of promise, having no hope and without God in the world. But now in Christ Jesus you who once were far off have been *brought near* by the blood of Christ. (Ephesians 2:1–13, *emphasis added*)

Paul refers to the Ephesians prior to their conversion as "dead." Just as Lazarus, who had been dead for four days, did not come out of the tomb until Jesus spoke and raised him to life (John 11) neither do we rise from spiritual death until the Lord Jesus, speaking through the Spirit's Word, raises us to spiritual life. Now consider these Bible passages.

I bow my knees before the Father . . . that according to the riches of His glory *He may grant you to be strengthened* with power through His Spirit in your inner being, so that Christ may dwell in your hearts through faith. (Ephesians 3:14, 16–17, *emphasis added*)

Therefore whoever disregards this, disregards not man but God, who *gives* His Holy Spirit to you. (1 Thessalonians 4:8, *emphasis added*)

For we ourselves were once foolish, disobedient, led astray, and slaves to various passions and pleasures, passing our days in malice and envy, hated by others and hating one another. But when the goodness and loving kindness of God our Savior appeared, He saved us, not because of works done by us in righteousness, but according to His own mercy, by the washing of regeneration and renewal of the Holy Spirit, whom He *poured out* on us richly through Jesus Christ our Savior, so that being justified by his *grace* we might become heirs according to the hope of eternal life. The saying is trustworthy. (Titus 3:3–8)

The Bible clearly teaches that the Holy Spirit is given *to* us, not grasped *by* us. The Holy Spirit is given to us in and with the Word of the Gospel, which He then uses to create faith in us. Thus faith is God's gift, not our work, and we become God's children not by our choice but by His. When

we know this truth, the terrible burden of obligation is removed from us
so we may live confidently before
God, knowing that despite our failings
and inability, we are God's children
through His grace in Jesus Christ.

*Faith is God's gift,
not our work.*

In *The Proper Distinction between Law and Gospel*, C. F. W. Walther states clearly that faith is not something for which we can take credit. Thesis 14 of his book reads: "In the tenth place, the Word of God is not rightly divided when faith is required as a condition of justification and salvation, as if a person were righteous in the sight of God and saved, not only by faith, but also on account of his faith, for the sake of his faith, and in view of his faith."[25] In explanation of this thesis, Walther writes:

> What God's Word really means when it says that man is justified and saved by faith alone is nothing else than this: Man is *not saved by his own acts*, but *solely* by the doing and dying of his Lord and Savior Jesus Christ, the Redeemer of the whole world. Over against this teaching modern theologians assert that in the salvation of man two kinds of activity must be noted: in the first place, there is something that God must do. His part is the most difficult, for He must accomplish the task of redeeming men. But in the second place, something is required that man must do. For it will not do to admit persons to

heaven, after they have been redeemed, without fur-
ther parley [talk]. Man must do something really
great—he has to believe. This teaching overthrows
the Gospel completely.[26]

In the Christian faith, glory is given to God, not to
man. For example, in the First Article of the Apostles' Creed,
God receives the glory for the creation of heaven and earth.
Who would be fool enough to take credit for that? In the
same way, in the Second Article of the Apostles' Creed, God
receives the glory for salvation. After all, we had nothing to
do with God sending His Son into the world, except that our
sin made it necessary for Jesus to suffer such humiliation,
pain, and death. Although Satan may subvert and destroy
our faith at any point, he frequently focuses on the Third
Article of the Apostles' Creed to convince us that in the area
of faith and conversion there is something we contribute.
But as Lutherans, indeed, as Christians, we insist that also in
the area of faith and conversion all glory must be given to
God alone. Only the Holy Spirit can create faith, which He
does by showing us Jesus.

How the Spirit shows us Jesus may be better understood if we consider the nature of faith. Because many people misunderstand what faith is, they have concluded that we
decide to become Christians, that we make a decision for
Jesus, and that this decision is instrumental in becoming a
child of God. But if this is so and if it is also true that we are
justified by faith, those who teach these things also are teach-

ing that we are at least partially responsible for our own jus-tification. But what exactly is faith? Lutherans frequently use the word *trust* to describe the nature of faith or as a syn-onym for the word *faith*. Who creates trust? The one who trusts or the one who is trusted?

Many years ago, my 4-month-old son Dirk was lying on the couch when his oldest brother, Seth, began to play with him. Seth hugged and kissed Dirk, who cooed and smiled. Then Seth left. A few moments later, my daughter Kirsten walked up to the sofa to spend time with her little brother. Before Kirsten even touched Dirk, he began to whine and whimper. Kirsten, who was 3 years old, hadn't yet learned how to be gentle with a baby. Dirk didn't enjoy being rolled over or dragged around by the arm. Although Kirsten had no desire to hurt him, Dirk didn't trust Kirsten. Dirk cooed and smiled for Seth because he trusted Seth to treat him gently and carefully. Did Dirk make a decision to trust Seth and not Kirsten? Did he decide to trust boys but not girls? Did he decide to trust 9-year-olds but not 3-year-olds? No, trust in his brother was created in Dirk by Seth's behav-ior and distrust in Kirsten was caused by her behavior.

As another example, how would you react if a politi-cian who has not shared his platform with you says, "I only have your best interests at heart. Trust me." Would you trust him immediately? No, he needs to earn your trust, which he does on the basis of the way he acts. If you come to trust this politician, it will be because he has acted in a trustworthy fashion. It is the nature of trust that it can be created only by the one who is trusted.

The same is true of faith. It can be created only by the one who is believed. The message about Jesus—who He is, what He has done for us—is the message that brings us to faith in God. The Holy Spirit shows us Jesus, how much He loved us, how He sacrificed Himself for us, how His passion for His wandering sheep was so great that He, the Good Shepherd, gave up His life for the sheep. The Holy Spirit shows us how trustworthy the Savior is, and faith is the result. Thus faith is created by the Spirit through His Word. Because of faith, we are justified, we enter the kingdom of God, and we enter the church. This is how we come to Mount Zion, the city of the living God, the heavenly Jerusalem. This is how we come into fellowship with an uncountable company of angels, with those whose names are written in the Book of Life, and with God our Father and with Jesus, His Son.

Because we cannot stand on Mount Sinai and survive God's judgment, God the Son takes on our human flesh and does everything necessary for our salvation. Jesus takes on Mount Sinai and lives a holy life. He marches to Mount Calvary, endures our shame and guilt, bears our death and punishment, washes our sins away, and rises again to life so we might be justified. By showing us Christ's work at Sinai and Calvary, the Holy Spirit brings us to Mount Zion where as baptized, forgiven, and believing children of God, we live every moment under God's mercy and love. In Zion, we are declared justified, righteous, and holy in God's eyes. On Mount Zion our lives are restored so we may "live under Him in His kingdom and serve Him in everlasting righteousness, innocence, and blessedness."[27]

What does it mean to be citizens of this kingdom called Zion? God says: "For Zion's sake I will not keep silent, and for Jerusalem's sake I will not be quiet until her righteousness goes forth as brightness, and her salvation as a burning torch" (Isaiah 62:1). As residents of Zion, God is on our side. He stands before us to protect us from any danger we might encounter. He stands behind us to guard against temptations or harm that might otherwise overtake us unexpectedly. He stands up for us to speak on our behalf and to vindicate us in the face of shame or accusation of any kind. He holds us, lifts us up, and saves us from the flood of troubles that threatens to overwhelm us. He stands as a solid rock beneath us.

> This I believe, yea rather, in this I make my
>   boast,
> That God is my dear Father, the Friend who
>   loves me most;
> And that whate'er betide me, My Savior is at
>   hand
> Through stormy seas to guide me And bring
>   me safe to land.[28]

CHAPTER THREE

WE ARE ALIVE

The father of a pastor friend of mine was dying of cancer. Those who have experienced the battle with cancer know that it takes its emotional and spiritual toll on the family. At first this pastor did his best to share God's Word and to pray with his own family, as he would have done with any family in his congregation. As the disease progressed, however, it became more difficult to do so. The emotions and pain were too much for my friend, and he could not get through a reading or sing a hymn with his family. As we talked about this, I reminded my friend that his congregation had called him to be a pastor, but his family had not. God had called him to be a son, a brother, a father, and a husband. In each of these relationships, God was at work to help the family members serve one another as they faced this trial.

We know that God has called us by name in Baptism and washed away our sins. We know that by faith we are holy. There is another calling given to each person—that of Christian vocation, which is a holy calling. As Gene Veith puts it, vocation is the divinity of daily life.[1] It is in the daily life of the baptized that God shows love to the family and to the world. In crucial moments such as a family member's fight with cancer, many of the vocations into which God has called us become clear. Martin Luther states that God has appointed many different stations or offices in life so the love of Jesus may be made manifest.[2] When we love our neighbor, we love Jesus. When we serve our neighbor, we serve Jesus. When we do the tasks God gives us to do, our actions show love for God and glorify Him.

Our calling or vocation in life has been cleansed by the blood of the Lamb. Everything we do is holy by faith in Christ. The Christian moves from the call of Baptism in the church to the baptismal call in daily life. The worship of daily life is to love our neighbor through all the offices God gives to us, which begins with the responsibility of the Fourth Commandment: "Honor your father and your mother" (Exodus 20:12). Thus the office of parent becomes the foundation for every other station in life. Society flows from the family, as do the good works that God has called us to do.

According to God's Word, in God's eyes only believers

do a good work. Only the deed done in faith is acceptable. "For whatever does not proceed from faith is sin" (Romans 14:23b). Even our finest and most honorable deed in this life must be cleansed by the blood of the Lamb. For example, consider two teenage boys who live by an elderly widow. Bill, an unbeliever, visits her often, runs errands gladly, and does yard work even without being asked. On the other hand, John, a Christian, must be threatened by his father with loss of car privileges before he will mow the lawn, which he does grudgingly. In this scenario, who did the good work? The answer is John, the Christian. His deed is good only because his faith in Jesus cleansed it, despite John's motivation (the possibility of being grounded). Bill's deed is exactly the deed that damns him because it is not done in faith and perhaps is motivated by the belief that God should give him credit for doing something nice.

St. Paul described the spiritual condition of the Ephesian congregation before faith in this way: "You were dead in the trespasses and sins in which you once walked" (Ephesians 2:1–2). However, Paul added: "But God, being rich in mercy, because of the great love with which He loved us, even when we were dead in our trespasses, made us alive together with Christ—by grace you have been saved—and raised us up with Him and seated us with Him in the heavenly places in Christ Jesus" (Ephesians 2:4–6). Believers are alive. Just as Jesus raised Lazarus from the dead (John 11), so He has raised us. Just as Jesus rose from death to life, God

Faith is a vibrant, living thing.

has raised us from spiritual death to spiritual life.

Jesus says, "Apart from Me you can do nothing" (John 15:5), but He also says, "I am the vine; you are the branches. Whoever abides in Me and I in him, he it is that bears much fruit" (John 15:5). Apart from Christ, there is no such thing as a good work in God's eyes. The writer to the Hebrews says: "Without faith it is impossible to please [God]" (Hebrews 11:6). In Christ, Christians constantly please God with the works that flow out of faith. Thus St. Paul says: "I can do all things through Him who strengthens me" (Philippians 4:13).

The faith of a Christian is not a cold, intellectual understanding of facts. Faith is created by God. Therefore, faith is a vibrant, living thing. Faith certainly includes the understanding of various facts explained in Scripture, but faith is more than just understanding. Faith is trust in God. Faith is love for God. Faith is a desire to be with God. Faith is faithful to the one who has been so kind, good, and gracious to us. Faith brings us into the family of God. It involves our relationship to our Father through the work of His Son. As a son or daughter of the Father, our relationship with our loving and gracious heavenly Father is made perfect and complete once again.

Because of its beauty, the authors of the Formula of Concord, one of our Lutheran Confessions, included the following quotation from Luther's description of faith in his preface to the Book of Romans:

> Faith is a divine work in us that transforms us and begets us anew from God, kills the Old Adam, makes us entirely different people in heart, spirit, mind, and all our powers, and brings the Holy Spirit with it. Oh, faith is a living, busy, active, mighty thing, so that it is impossible for it not to be constantly doing what is good. Likewise, faith does not ask if good works are to be done, but before one can ask, faith has already done them and is constantly active. Whoever does not perform such good works is a faithless man, blindly tapping around in search of faith and good works without knowing what either faith or good works are, and in the meantime he chatters and jabbers a great deal about faith and good works. Faith is a vital, deliberate trust in God's grace, so certain that it would die a thousand times for it. And such confidence and knowledge of divine grace makes us joyous, mettlesome, and merry toward God and all creatures. This the Holy Spirit works by faith, and therefore without any coercion a man is willing and desirous to do good to everyone, to serve everyone, to suffer everything for the love of God and to his glory, who has been so gracious to him. It is therefore as impossible to separate works from faith as it is to separate heat and light from fire.[3]

According to Luther, faith is dynamic. It expresses itself in words and actions. Faith expresses itself in love. Good works can never save, but true faith never exists without them. Even then, it is the Holy Spirit who creates the good works.

According to God's Word, there is an intimate connection between faith and life. The kind of life we live flows from the faith that lives in our hearts. As we grow and mature in what God wills for our lives, we learn better to love our neighbor. Good works will flow from the work of the Spirit in us. Some think that faith can be genuine without the Christian life that accompanies it. St. James says: "Show me your faith apart from your works, and I will show you my faith by my works. You believe that God is one; you do well. Even the demons believe—and shudder!" (James 2:18–19). In fact, the entire Epistle of James is required reading for those who believe they are God's children though they continue to embezzle, lie, fornicate, or persist in defying what they know to be God's will.

In his Epistle to the Romans, St. Paul explains how impossible it is for Christians to be complacent about their behavior.

> What shall we say then? Are we to continue in sin that grace may abound? By no means! How can we who died to sin still live in it? Do you not know that all of us who have been baptized into Christ Jesus were baptized into His death? We were buried therefore with Him by baptism into death, in order that, just as Christ was raised from the dead by the glory

of the Father, we too might walk in newness of life.
. . . So you also must consider yourselves dead to sin
and alive to God in Christ Jesus. Let not sin therefore
reign in your mortal bodies, to make you obey their
passions. (Romans 6:1–4, 11–12)

> *There is an intimate connection*
> *between faith and life.*

To die to sin means more, however, than simply that we
are forgiven. It also means that we now live to the glory of
God. Paul emphasizes that we used to be dead in our sins,
but now we are alive. To be forgiven means the sins that used
to accuse us can't accuse us anymore. They're dead. The sins
and the guilt that used to condemn us can't condemn us
anymore. They're dead. Paul says to the Romans: "We know
that our old self was crucified with Him in order that the
body of sin might be brought to nothing" (Romans 6:6).
Paul says almost the same thing to the Colossians: "[God
cancelled] the record of debt that stood against us with its
legal demands. This He set aside, nailing it to the cross"
(Colossians 2:14).

This forgiven life brings us the new life of holiness. We
do not have to be afraid of doing the right thing. Paul says to
the Romans: "Do not present your members to sin as instruments for unrighteousness, but present yourselves to God as
those who have been brought from death to life, and your

members to God as instruments for righteousness. For sin will have no dominion over you, since you are not under law but under grace" (Romans 6:13–14). Precisely because we have died to sin, we now worship and love God daily. We worship and love God daily as we love and serve our neighbors, our family members, even strangers. We look for ways to love our parents, to serve our neighbor, and to do the right thing at work. God's love actually frees us to love both Him and our neighbor.

Paul wants Christians to understand what it means to die to sin. It means that we now live for God. We love Him, we serve Him, and we want to make Him happy by doing what He asks of us. In our Baptism, we died to sin and were buried with Christ. We were born again and now live a new life in Him by faith. Through faith in Jesus, we have become the temple of the Holy Spirit (1 Corinthians 6:19). Christians live as children of God, members of His holy, redeemed, and sanctified family. Christians don't look at God's grace as an easy way into heaven that now allows us to live a life of sin. Instead, Christians thank and praise God for His grace as they demonstrate their love for God and neighbor.

Christians are always sinners and saints at the same time. We do not stop being sinful when we become Christians. The more we understand the Law, the more we realize we cannot live up to its demands for perfection. We need a Savior no less today than the day on which we were baptized. Christians live in a lifelong struggle with sin. After his conversion to Christianity, St. Paul acknowledged that a terrible battle continued to rage within himself.

> So I find it to be a law that when I want to do right, evil lies close at hand. For I delight in the law of God, in my inner being, but I see in my members another law waging war against the law of my mind and making me captive to the law of sin that dwells in my members. Wretched man that I am! Who will deliver me from this body of death? (Romans 7:21–24)

Every Christian goes through the same struggles as Paul. Temptations surround us daily. In fact, on the night He was betrayed, Jesus told His disciples to "watch and pray that you may not enter into temptation. The spirit indeed is willing, but the flesh is weak" (Matthew 26:40). Frequently, we fail in our struggle with temptation. We sin daily. But through faith in Jesus, we stand holy, pure, and innocent in God's eyes. We are like Paul, wretched in our inability to do what is right and at the same time rejoicing in the victory we have through Jesus Christ our Savior. We can thank Jesus for grace that is not cheap but precious, the grace that He bought with His precious blood, the grace that opens the gates of heaven and places us on Mount Zion. As residents of Mount Zion, we rejoice with saints and angels around the throne of God as we thank Him for the death of our old sinful nature and for our new life in Christ. We also ask God to give us the strength to live this new life to His glory.

Only God's love for us in Christ gives us the Christian life. In this sense Christians are unique in their relationship to God. All other religions offer salvation only to those who meet legal demands. Other religions present a god who punishes all those who break his rules and promises salvation only to those who keep all the rules. Adherents of these works-based religions live in constant spiritual anguish, never confident that their god loves them or accepts them. They are never sure their inner thoughts are pure enough. They are never sure their deeds have been done well enough. In such a religious life, obedience is rendered not out of love for their god but out of fear and the desire to avoid judgment and punishment.

Do we keep God's Law because He will damn us if we don't? No. God has washed away all our guilt through Christ, His Son. He will not damn us. Do we keep God's Law because we are afraid of what He will do to us if we don't? No. As St. Paul says: "There is therefore now no condemnation for those who are in Christ Jesus" (Romans 8:1). The center of the Christian faith is that God has punished Christ in our place. God is not angry with us because He truly loves us through Christ, His Son, and sees us as His dear children. We are now free to serve Him out of love. God has created love for Him and for His family, the church, in our hearts. The Gospel declares us holy, so now we see God's Law eye-to-eye and it does not kill us. We are free to live it.

The most important works Christians do are often the

simplest, performed as part of our daily life as God's children. I couldn't help but laugh one Sunday morning as I watched the offering plate arrive before a mother who had given her young son a quarter as a gift for Jesus. As she whispered that he should put it in the plate, he shook his head. She whispered more urgently as those to her right began to wonder about the progress of the offering plate. The young boy shook his head more vigorously. Finally, the mother shook the hand with the quarter until the coin fell into the plate. What a tremendous Christian deed. Her work has inestimable value. Certainly this woman did what moms sometimes have to do—she forced her son to do the right thing. Even Christian parents must do this. But this mother brought her child to church and was teaching him that everything comes from God and that we give back to God because we love Him and want to thank Him.

And we do love God. When the Holy Spirit brings us to faith, we are able to love the Father who would give His own Son out of love for us, the Son who sacrificed Himself so we could live forever, and the Spirit who has brought us such precious, life-giving news. When we see how greatly God has loved us, and truly believe that His love is for us, we cannot help but love God in return. At the center of this relationship of love between God and His people is Jesus. It is for Jesus' sake that the Father loves us, and it is because of what Jesus has done that we love the Father. Without the Savior, we could not and would not love God.

Love is born not out of condemnation but out of forgiveness, not out of terror but out of faith, not out of despair but out of hope. Only the message of forgiveness in Jesus creates faith, hope, and true love. It is difficult for preachers and laypeople, parents and children to grasp and live out the fact that only the Gospel creates love, not the Law. Only the message of Christ's work for us creates love for God in the hearts of Christians.

Thus Christians do not obey God because He demands love. Christians do not honor God because they will be damned if they don't. Christians do not serve God because they are afraid of His anger. Christians love and honor God because they are grateful for all He has done for them. Christians serve God because they take true joy in living for Him. Jesus is at the center of all we do and say because He took our sin on Himself, suffered for us, died for us, and rose for us. Because of Jesus, we love God. Because of Jesus, we love our neighbor. Because of Jesus, we serve both God and neighbor.

CHAPTER FOUR

MOUNT ZION
AND THE CROSS

I have said these things to you, that in Me you may have peace. In the world you will have tribulation. But take heart; I have overcome the world. (John 16:33)

"My soul is very sorrowful, even to death" (Matt. 26:38). Moreover, His battle against death and the devil had now reached its highest point. Here Christ richly poured out His great and heartfelt comfort, which is the property of all Christendom and which men should long for in all troubles and afflictions.[1]

---

*Joy and trouble go hand in hand
in the life of the Christian.*

Living in Zion is living the life of the cross. Because Zion understands life as it really is, Lutherans do not live in denial. Our Lord understands real human beings: We are sinners and saints at the same time (Romans 7:19ff.). We are holy by faith, but our thoughts, words, and deeds are immersed in sin. Thus Christians are always at war with themselves. This war is waged under the cross, but it brings pain, suffering, and hardship to Christians just as life brings the same to everyone who lives on earth.

There is a far more popular understanding of Zion promulgated today that is not found in the Scriptures. It is called a "theology of glory," which may also be called the believers' prosperity. One of the more popular preachers of the theology of glory is Norman Vincent Peale, who promotes the "power of positive thinking." According to this theology of glory, believers should expect material prosperity, success, affluence, victory, and triumph in all areas of daily life. And the more thoroughly one believes in God, trusts in Him, and yields to Him, the more successful, prosperous, and burden-free life will be. This is not a new message. It's an old message, one that turns faith into a work, then rewards the faithful for the work they have done. The theology of glory posits that if we are good to God, God will be good to us; if we are faithful to God, God will be faithful to us; if we follow God, worship God, and obey God, God will pay us our due.

Most of us were raised with what has come to be termed the Protestant work ethic: Work hard and you will get what you deserve. To many it seems to be a sensible and practical message. But this isn't true when it comes to how God blesses us. God doesn't give us everything we ask for or good health or money or success because we have enough faith. He is not a giant soda machine in the sky into which we deposit our prayers and automatically receive our desired answers because we prayed "hard enough."

Christians often have just as many problems as their nonbelieving neighbors—and sometimes more. Christians become sick. They are involved in accidents. They suffer pain, financial difficulty, failed marriages, dysfunctional families, disobedient and rebellious children, abusive spouses, apathetic parents. Christians must endure humiliation, shame, embarrassment, temptations that never seem to end, even persecution. In addition, Christians are troubled by sin, they struggle with sin. Any pastor will be able to describe innumerable encounters with sin, sickness, and sorrow in his ministry. Not only do pastors confront this daily as they work with parishioners, but professional church workers themselves are not immune to the ravages of sin in this world. Christians bleed and hurt and die just like everybody else, which is one reason Christians often are considered foolish and pathetic by nonbelievers. It's also why we who are Christians sometimes become discouraged.

In one of his letters to the Thessalonians, St. Paul touches on the great paradox that joy and trouble go hand in hand in the life of the Christian. Paul writes: "You received the word in much affliction, with the joy of the Holy Spirit" (1 Thessalonians 1:6). Although becoming a Christian brings the greatest joy a human being can experience, God does not promise us an end to trouble and suffering until our term on earth has ended. To the contrary, Jesus says, "If anyone would come after Me, let him deny himself and take up his cross and follow Me" (Matthew 16:24). Just as Jesus bore a cross when He came to save us, so we who follow Him also bear a cross.

What does Jesus say will happen to His disciples if they are faithful to Him? "But be on your guard. For they will deliver you over to councils and you will be beaten in the synagogues, and you will stand before governors and kings for My sake, to bear witness before them" (Mark 13:9). This "promise" was made not only to the twelve disciples but also to all who wish to follow Jesus. In His Sermon on the Mount, Jesus says: "Blessed are those who are persecuted for righteousness' sake, for theirs is the kingdom of heaven. Blessed are you when others revile you and persecute you and utter all kinds of evil against you falsely on My account. Rejoice and be glad, for your reward is great in heaven, for so they persecuted the prophets who were before you" (Matthew 5:10–12).

I will never forget the first time this truth became clear to me. I was working on an iron ore boat for U.S. Steel. I was 18 and just out of high school. A few weeks after I began work, I was sitting in the galley when Joe, one of the deck-hands, entered. An ex-convict with a reputation, Joe was drunk, mad, and looking for a fight. When he saw me, Joe insulted me, my mother, my father, my brothers and sisters, my looks, my abilities, and anything else he thought might get a rise out of me. When I did not take the bait, he began to insult Christianity. When I continued to remain silent, Joe specifically attacked my hope in Christ and concluded by saying, "Preacher, when you die, you're goin' to the same place I'm goin' and everybody else is goin'—six feet under. There ain't no hell and there ain't no heaven. You're goin' six feet under and that's where you're gonna stay!"

When it was apparent Joe was done, I said, "Joe, some-time when you're sober, I would be happy to talk to you about any of the things that are on your mind." Joe looked at me, turned around, and walked out of the galley.

Joe and I never talked, but the chief cook, who had wit-nessed the event, took me aside and said, "It took me forty years to learn to do what you just did. Anytime you want to talk to me, I will be happy to listen." The cook and I talked frequently after that.

Christians will be persecuted, made fun of, ostracized,

or penalized in some way. When we live as Christians, we bear a cross as Jesus did. At the same time, God uses these crosses for our benefit and the benefit of others. Sometimes it is difficult to see this, especially when the crosses are not the result of our Christian testimony but are placed on us by God for reasons that are not readily apparent. God may place burdens on us to accomplish His will for us and for others. Sometimes these crosses are particularly difficult for us to accept and to understand. For example, as a pastor I called on a homebound woman named Betty who suffered from diabetes. The disease had claimed her eyesight, and both legs had been amputated above the knees. Her husband had abandoned her, and her only son, with whom she lived, was on drugs. During one visit, Betty asked why God allowed her to live. "What good am I, Pastor?" she asked. "I can't help anybody. My life has no purpose. Why doesn't God just take me? Why does He make me live like this?"

My heart went out to her, but I was prepared to give her an answer. "Betty, every Sunday you are in church, and every time we have Communion, your neighbor Lloyd wheels you to the front of the church to receive the Sacrament. Do you know how your example strengthens them? They know your trials and your troubles, yet they see you continuing in the faith, week after week, always trusting in the Lord, like Job. Do you know how many of them are praying, 'Dear God, give me a faith like Betty's'?"

What I told Betty was true. God used her to strengthen

the faith of others. God always has a purpose in the crosses He places on us. Sometimes the greatest cross is His apparent absence. We look at events around us and we are tempted to ask where Jesus is. We recall the collapse of the World Trade Center and cannot avoid wondering where God was for those people, especially for those who trusted in Him. When we read of violence in Africa or the Middle East, especially violence against Christians, we question whether Jesus cares. This world and what goes on in it severely challenges our faith. The world seems to mock us constantly, taunting, "Look at you Christians. You think you're special. But you get sick and suffer and die just like everybody else. Where is He, this Jesus in whom you trust? He said He'd help you. Where is He?" We may grow confused and our faith may be shaken as we are attacked by constant physical pain, devastating emotional pain, broken relationships, bankruptcy, loss of hope, anger, bitterness, stress, sorrow, and the list goes on and on. Where is God's plan in all this? Finally, we cry out for God's help, which puts us in good company. In many of the psalms, we hear God's people crying out to Him in anguished expressions of pain, distress, and misery. Consider these examples:

> O LORD, why do You cast my soul away? Why do You hide Your face from me? (Psalm 88:14)

> How long, O LORD? Will You be angry forever? (Psalm 79:5)

Will the LORD spurn forever, never again be favorable? Has His steadfast love forever ceased? Are His promises at an end for all time? Has God forgotten to be gracious? Has He in anger shut up His compassion? (Psalm 77:7–9)

God does not abandon us.

As a pastor stands at the foot of a hospital bed or meets with someone whose marriage is dissolving or counsels someone whose spouse has died, he often hears the questions Why? and Where is God's love? and Where is God's mercy? Thankfully, God answers these questions. St. Paul comforts the Corinthians with these words: "No temptation has overtaken you that is not common to man. God is faithful, and He will not let you be tempted beyond your ability, but with the temptation He will also provide the way of escape, that you may be able to endure it" (1 Corinthians 10:13). God does not abandon us. He knows what we are experiencing. In fact, His own Son has experienced these same problems and temptations. The writer to the Hebrews says about Jesus: "For we do not have a high priest who is unable to sympathize with our weaknesses, but one who in every respect has been tempted as we are, yet without sin. Let us then with confidence draw near to the throne of grace, that we may receive mercy and find grace to help in time of need" (Hebrews 4:15–16).

Jesus, our high priest, knows and understands our weaknesses. He will hear our prayers and answer us. Jesus says: "Ask, and it will be given to you; seek, and you will find; knock, and it will be opened to you. For everyone who asks receives, and the one who seeks finds, and to the one who knocks it will be opened" (Matthew 7:7–8). These are not empty promises of hope. These are the true words of the Son of God. He knows what we need and what is best for us. Life is not luck, it is not random. Life is a gift from God, and He sustains and provides for all our needs. God watches over us, protects us, and provides for us. He hears our anguished cries for help, our prayers of need. He loves us and says, "I am with you always, to the end of the age" (Matthew 28:20). God invites us to call on Him in the day of trouble, as any child would call on his father for help (Psalm 50:15).

We may not always understand God's answers, so He points us to the day when all suffering will end. He reminds us that we are pilgrims on this earth (1 Peter 2:11) who look forward to an incorruptible inheritance reserved in heaven for us (1 Peter 1:4). And God reminds us through the apostle Paul that "the sufferings of this present time are not worth comparing with the glory that is to be revealed to us" (Romans 8:18). But the answer to our suffering does not only lie in our future salvation. God promises us through the apostle Paul that "for those who love God all things work together for good, for those who are called according to His purpose" (Romans 8:28). God uses our suffering and weakness to drive us to confess our helplessness before Him, which then drives us to Jesus.

Even as Christians, our sinful flesh continues to tempt us to believe that we can do without God's grace, without His mercy, without Christ. The devil tries to seduce us away from Mount Calvary and send us back to Mount Sinai. He tempts us to trust our own abilities. But God loves us, so He shows us our weaknesses and places crosses on us to return us to Calvary, to cause us to cry out daily to Him for mercy. This is the baptized life of the Christian. As baptized children of God, we know we are "called according to His purpose" (Romans 8:28). Jesus is always the answer to the questions and prayers of every Christian. Through the crosses He places on those He loves, God assures that His children will never stop looking to Jesus as Savior. Our Lutheran Confessions put it this way:

> Scripture explains that Job's afflictions were not imposed on him because of his past misdeeds. So afflictions are not always punishments or signs of wrath. When in the midst of troubles terrified consciences see only God's punishment and wrath, they should not feel that God has rejected them but they should be taught that troubles have other and more important purposes. They should look at these other and more important purposes, that God is doing his alien work in order to do his proper work, as Isaiah teaches in a long sermon in his twenty-

eighth chapter. . . . Therefore troubles are not always penalties for certain past deeds, but works of God, intended for our profit, that the power of God might be made more manifest in our weakness.[2]

Luther touches on the same theme in his explanation of John 15:1–2 in which Jesus says, "I am the true vine, and My Father is the vinedresser. Every branch of Mine that does not bear fruit He takes away, and every branch that does bear fruit He prunes, that it may bear more fruit." In describing Christians as the vine, Luther says:

> Here Christ does not present a useless, unfruitful tree to our view. No, He presents the precious vine, which bears much fruit and produces the sweetest and most delicious juice, even though it does not delight the eye. He interprets all the suffering which both He and they are to experience as nothing else than the diligent work and care which a vinedresser expends on his vines and their branches to make them grow and bear abundantly. With these words Christ wants to teach us to have a view of the affliction and suffering of Christians that is far different from what appears on the surface and before the world. He says that Christians are not afflicted without God's counsel and will; that when this does happen, it is a sign of grace and fatherly love, not of wrath and punishment, and must serve our welfare.

This requires the art of believing and being sure

that whatever hurts and distresses us does not happen to hurt or harm us but for our good and profit. We must compare this to the work of a vinedresser who hoes and cultivates his vine. If the vine were able to be aware of this, could talk, and saw the vinedresser coming along and chopping about its roots with his mattock or his hoe and cutting the wood from its branches with his clipper or his pruning hook, it would be prompted by what it saw and felt to say: "Ah, what are you doing? Now I must wither and decay, for you are removing the soil from my roots and are belaboring my branches with those iron teeth. You are tearing and pinching me everywhere, and I will have to stand in the ground bare and seared. You are treating me more cruelly than one treats any tree or plant." But the vinedresser would reply: "You are a fool and do not understand. For even if I do cut a branch from you, it is a totally useless branch; it takes away your strength and your sap. Then the other branches, which should bear fruit, must suffer. Therefore away with it! This is for your own good." You say: "But I do not understand it, and I have a different feeling about it." The vinedresser declares: "But I understand it well. I am doing this for your welfare, to keep the foreign and wild branches from sucking out the strength and the sap of the others. Now you will be able to yield more and better fruit and to produce good wine." The same thing is true when the vinedresser applies manure to the stock of the vine; this, too, he does for the benefit of the vine even though the vine might complain again and say: "What, pray, is this for? Is it not enough that you are hacking and cutting me to pieces? Now with this filthy cow manure, which is intolerable in the barn and elsewhere, you are defiling my tender branches, which yield such delicious juice! Must I stand for this too?"

That is how Christ interprets the suffering which He and His Christians are to endure on earth. This is to be a benefaction and a help rather than affliction and harm. Its purpose is to enable them to bear all the better fruit and all the more.[3]

The crosses Christians bear are sent by God not only for the benefit of the one who bears the cross but also for the benefit of others. Christians need to remember that we are all members of one church. We are family—God's family. And what do family members do for one another? They help one another. Thus the crosses God places on His children provide Christian brothers and sisters with opportunities to show one another their love. Such acts of love are multiplied in the lives of millions of Christians countless times each day.

In his first letter to the Corinthians, St. Paul teaches that Christians are members of the body of Christ, who is the head of the church. Paul tells us that "there may be no division in the body, but that the members may have the same care for one another. If one member suffers, all suffer together; if one member is honored, all rejoice together. Now you are the body of Christ and individually members of it" (1 Corinthians 12:25–27). Thus the crosses God sends us, as well as the joys, are meant to bless the entire family of God. Therefore, we can sing:

> Blest be the tie that binds
> Our hearts in Christian love;
> The unity of heart and mind
> Is like to that above.
>
> Before our Father's throne
> We pour our ardent prayers;
> Our fears, our hopes, our aims are one,
> Our comforts and our cares.
>
> We share our mutual woes,
> Our mutual burdens bear,
> And often for each other flows
> The sympathizing tear.[4]

Christians live together on Mount Zion as one family—brothers and sisters in Christ, who is our head. As members of the same family, we rejoice in helping one another. Our joy grows when we see how our Lord looks at our works of love for others. Jesus describes what God will say to His people on the Day of Judgment.

Then the King will say to those on His right, "Come, you who are blessed by My Father, inherit the kingdom prepared for you from the foundation of the world. For I was hungry and you gave Me food, I was thirsty and you gave Me drink, I was a stranger and you welcomed Me, I was naked and you clothed Me, I was sick and you visited Me, I was in prison and you came to Me." Then the righteous will answer Him, saying, "Lord, when did we see You hungry and feed You, or thirsty and give You drink? When did we see You a stranger and welcome You, or naked and clothe You? When did we see You sick or in prison and visit You?" The King will answer them, "Truly, I say to you, as you did it to one of the least of these My brothers, you did it to Me." (Matthew 25:34–40)

Thus in showing love to other Christians, in helping them bear their crosses, we show our love for Jesus. As we patiently bear the crosses that God has placed on us, we become more like Christ, who bore a cross for all the world and in bearing that cross redeemed us.

In Jesus is the final and strongest answer to all our questions about the crosses we bear. When we suffer and can see no good in our suffering, no reason in our pain, no purpose in our anguish, the Holy Spirit leads us once more to look to Jesus. Who could have imagined that God could bring such good from such suffering? Surely those who followed Jesus did not think so. Undoubtedly, they saw Jesus suffering and dying and wondered why, as the Son of God, He didn't stop suffering, leave the cross, and avoid death. Yet out of apparent defeat came victory—victory over sin, death, hell, and all that could hurt us. The cross of suffering has become a sign for all Christians, a sign of salvation, hope, and everlasting life. Just as God brought the greatest possible good out of the greatest possible suffering, so will He also cause all things to "work together for good, for those who are the called according to His purpose" (Romans 8:28).

On the outside, Zion appears to be no different from the rest of this world. However, the world cannot see faith. Thus Zion possesses a rich life and a righteousness the world does not know. God, who gives this life and righteousness to Zion will not remain silent about it. Instead, He will proclaim His message throughout creation, a message of comfort to Zion, a message of joy about Zion. Of course, this message centers in Jesus our Savior. When we look to Jesus, we see a baby and know that He does not come to frighten us but to draw us to Himself in love. When we look to Jesus, we see His temptation in the wilderness and know that He does not come to intimidate us with threats of punishment for sin and failure. He understands our temptations because He has experienced them, and He comes to love and comfort us. When we look to Jesus, we see Him in the Garden of Gethsemane in such anguish that He sweats drops of blood. We see Him whipped and crowned with thorns, suffering great pain on the cross, and finally dying. Thus we are assured that Jesus knows our pain. Ultimately, we see Jesus bearing the guilt and sin of the whole world on that cross and know that He understands our shame. But Christ has removed our shame and guilt. He has conquered death for us. Now He gives everything that is His to us: His life of perfection, His conquest of sin and temptation, His death that pays for all guilt, His resurrection and life. All these are the possession of Zion. Christ is the bridegroom and Zion is the bride, and to her He gives all that He possesses.

We are His righteous ones.

Zion hears and believes this message, and Zion is born, is justified, and lives. Now God says about Zion: "I will not keep silent . . . until her righteousness goes forth as brightness and her salvation as a burning torch" (Isaiah 62:1). God rejoices in His precious bride, the church, and goes to great lengths to protect her and to establish her in the world. He will give her all she needs to shine in this world of darkness. As a demonstration of His love, God calls Zion "a crown of beauty in the hand of the LORD, a royal diadem in the hand of your God" (Isaiah 62:3). That's what God says about those of us who through faith have been justified and made one with Christ. We are His precious people whom He has called out of darkness into His marvelous light. We are His righteous ones.

Through faith in Christ, we are His Zion.

Therefore, those of us who live on Mount Zion, who receive our life from Mount Calvary, should pray that our Father in heaven would deliver us from the temptations of this world. If we should succumb to these temptations, they would lead us to the foot of Mount Sinai where we would stand alone under God's Law. But St. Paul says: "By works of the law no human being will be justified in His sight, since through the law comes knowledge of sin" (Romans 3:20). Rather, we should keep our eyes on Jesus, "the founder and perfecter of our faith, who for the joy that was set before Him endured the cross, despising the shame, and is seated at the right hand of the throne of God" (Hebrews 12:2). We also should pray that we never tire of confessing that

> Christ alone is our salvation,
> Christ the rock on which we stand;
> Other than this sure foundation
> Will be found but sinking sand.
> Christ, His cross and resurrection,
> Is alone the sinner's plea.
> At the throne of God's perfection
> Nothing else can set him free.[5]

CHAPTER FIVE

MOUNT ZION
AND THE SACRAMENTS

We cannot leave our discussion of Mount Zion without giving full attention to the Gospel treasures that God has given to all who dwell on Zion, namely, the sacraments—Baptism and the Lord's Supper. Lutherans speak of the Word and Sacraments as God's means of grace. In our discussion of Mount Calvary and Mount Zion, we already have focused much attention on the message of the Gospel and how in it the Holy Spirit shows people Mount Calvary to bring them to Mount Zion. Now we will look at God's other means of grace—Baptism and the Lord's Supper.

Many people do not fully grasp the eternal comfort

The Sacraments are the Gospel.

and precious gifts the Lord provided when He gave the sacraments to Zion. Too often people see Baptism and Holy Communion primarily as pious acts of obedience that Christians perform out of love for their Lord. In fact, such a view transforms these sacraments into precisely the opposite of what they are. The sacraments are not prescribed works of piety that Christians are to perform for God or two more commandments added to the second table of the Law. The sacraments are grace. The sacraments are the Gospel. The sacraments are forgiveness given, salvation, and life. They are not what we do for Jesus; they are what Jesus does for us. The sacraments bestow on those who receive them all the benefits Jesus earned in His life, death, and resurrection. The sacraments focus on Jesus Christ.

HOLY BAPTISM

One evening I received a call from a new mother. When I had visited her and her first child in the hospital, they both were doing well, but now the child was sick. Although the doctors assured her and her husband that their daughter would get better, they were concerned. When I visited the couple in their home, they asked if they should baptize their baby now rather than await my return from a planned vacation. Although I consider it a wonderful experience for a congregation to witness a Baptism, I encouraged these parents to baptize their baby immediately. We held a brief service in which the little girl became God's child and an heir of eternal life.

The day before I was to leave on vacation, the father called to say that his daughter was doing much better. He seemed almost disappointed that they had gone ahead with the Baptism because they would have loved to do it in church. But while I was on vacation, I received a phone call to tell me the baby had died. The parents were grief stricken, but their sorrow was tempered by the knowledge that their daughter was with her Savior in heaven. Salvation had come to their child.

In the last chapter of his Gospel, Matthew describes Jesus' gift of Baptism: "All authority in heaven and on earth has been given to Me. Go therefore and make disciples of all nations, bap-

Baptism brings us into God's kingdom.

tizing them in the name of the Father and of the Son and of the Holy Spirit, teaching them to observe all that I have commanded you. And behold, I am with you always, to the end of the age" (Matthew 28:18–20). In these words, Jesus tells His church how to make disciples—baptize and teach. The sequence of Jesus words is interesting. He does not say "teach and baptize"; instead, Jesus says "baptize and teach." Normally, Baptism precedes teaching because God wants people to enter His kingdom as soon as possible. Baptism brings us into God's kingdom by forgiving our sin, covering us with God's grace, and creating faith in us. Because babies cannot yet understand instruction, the teaching comes later. Of course, in the case of adults who are able to understand, instruction comes first.

Some churches refuse to baptize babies and young children. Frequently, the denial of Baptism to infants is closely connected to the denial of original sin because those who do not baptize babies say these children are not sinful and do not need God's forgiveness. Others consider Baptism to be primarily an act of commitment the believer makes to God, a commitment infants and children are unable to make. However, Baptism is an act of God toward people in which He bestows His grace on sinful human beings. All people are sinful, including babies. Therefore, all people need Baptism.

God's Word is quite clear when it describes who is to be baptized and what Baptism does. Jesus says in Matthew 28 that "all nations" are to be baptized, which does not exclude children. Imagine your house is burning and you tell the firefighter your entire family is in the house. If the firefighter rescues your spouse and returns to working the hose, you'll be seriously alarmed. If the firefighter says that you didn't specifically mention children, you will point out that the concept of *family* includes children. In the same way, the concept of *nations* includes children. There is no reason to deny this precious Sacrament of Holy Baptism to children unless one believes they have no need of salvation. To say they have no need, however, denies original sin. How anyone who has had children can conclude they are not sinful seems impossible, but if personal experience does not convince us, we can turn to the words of King David: "Behold, I was brought forth in iniquity, and in sin did my mother conceive me" (Psalm 51:5). And Jesus said, "That which is born of the flesh is flesh" (John 3:6). The word *flesh* is used in Scripture to describe our sinful human nature. Children, too, are "born of the flesh." Therefore, it is wrong to deny the benefits of Baptism to children because it steals the mercy and grace of God from little children, who need it as much as any of us.

St. Peter seems to have anticipated that one day people would deny Baptism to young children. In the Book of Acts, which records the events of Pentecost, we are told that many who heard Peter's sermon that day were shocked by his description of their sinful condition. They asked, "Brothers, what shall we do?" (Acts 2:37). Peter answered: "Repent and be baptized every one of you in the name of Jesus Christ for the forgiveness of your sins, and you will receive the gift of the Holy Spirit. For the promise is for you and for your children and for all who are far off, everyone whom the Lord our God calls to Himself" (Acts 2:37–39). Not only did Peter indicate that "every one of you" should be baptized, but, in case they should misunderstand, he stated that the "promise is for you and for your children."

In Acts 16, we are told about the baptism of Lydia and

her household. There is no indication that children were excluded. In the same chapter, we read that Paul and Silas baptized the jailer at Philippi "and all his family" (Acts 16:33). Again, there is no indication that children or infants were excluded. In fact, there is no indication anywhere in the New Testament that babies or children are not to be baptized and that the blessings of this precious Sacrament are not meant for them.

What are the blessings of Baptism? Peter told his hearers on Pentecost: "Be baptized every one of you in the name of Jesus Christ for the forgiveness of your sins, and you will receive the gift of the Holy Spirit" (Acts 2:38). In Baptism, our sins are forgiven, God gives us His Holy Spirit, and we are saved. In describing his own Baptism, St. Paul states that Ananias urged him, "Now why do you wait? Rise and be baptized and wash away your sins" (Acts 22:16). Jesus says in the Gospel of Mark, "Whoever believes and is baptized will be saved" (Mark 16:16). St. Peter teaches the same thing in his first letter: "Baptism which corresponds to [the flood], now saves you . . . through the resurrection of Jesus Christ" (1 Peter 3:21).

How does Baptism save us? It applies to us the forgiveness Jesus earned for us on the cross. The apostle Paul uses a fascinating illustration in his Epistle to the Romans to demonstrate that Baptism actually brings forgiveness: "Do you not know that all of us who have been baptized into Christ Jesus were baptized into His death? We were buried

We were baptized into the death of Jesus.

therefore with Him by baptism into death, in order that, just as Christ was raised from the dead by the glory of the Father, we too might walk in newness of life" (Romans 6:3–4). What does Paul mean when he says we were baptized with Jesus into His death? Why did the Son of God take on human flesh and come to this earth? He did so to take our place under God's Law, to bear our sin and punishment, and, under God's curse, to die the death that should have been ours. He did all this to take away our sin. That's what John the Baptist said about Jesus: "Behold, the Lamb of God, who takes away the sin of the world!" (John 1:29). Baptism into Jesus' death means that our sins are taken away because we have died with Him. Thus every time we see a Baptism, we are to remember that we have died to sin and are forgiven. Just as the waters of the flood buried all the people of Noah's day except eight, so our sinful selves have been buried beneath the waters of Baptism and have been drowned and died. When we were baptized, we were baptized into the death of Jesus, and as He rose from death to a life of glory, we, too, will rise to a glorious new life. That life begins on this earth when our old sinful self has been put to death and buried in the waters of Baptism. This new life is one of forgiveness in which everything that could have accused and condemned us has been killed and can no

longer touch us. We stand absolutely holy, pure, and innocent before our God.

The account of Jesus' own baptism helps us understand
what Baptism does for us, but most people do not understand its depth. Christians typically may focus on the
Father's pleasure with Jesus, which is an important theme.
Or maybe they reflect on how this account demonstrates the
doctrine of the Trinity—the Father speaking from heaven
about His Son, who is on earth, and the Holy Spirit descending from heaven in the form of a dove. Or maybe the focus is
placed on the Father's statement that Jesus is His Son. These
are important facts to know, but we cannot fully appreciate
the account of Jesus' baptism unless we know what it has to
do with us personally—and this story has a great deal to do
with each of us. After all, as we learned when considering the
concept of substitution, everything Jesus did—including His
baptism—He did for us, not for Himself. In fact, Jesus didn't
need to be baptized. He didn't need to be born or die, either.
But Jesus didn't do any of these things for Himself. He did
them all for us, even as He was baptized on our behalf.

When we understand that Jesus' baptism was for us, it
takes on a whole new meaning. As we hear the Father's voice
say, "This is My beloved Son, with whom I am well pleased"
(Matthew 3:17), we realize that God the Father is talking not
only about Jesus but also about each of us. When we envi-
sion the Holy Spirit descending from heaven in the form of a
dove, we know that because Jesus was our substitute, the

Holy Spirit is meant for each of us. When we were baptized into Christ, everything that is Christ's became ours. This is what Paul stated when he wrote to the Romans. In his Epistle to the Colossians, Paul says almost the same thing: "Having been buried with Him in baptism, in which you were also raised with Him" (Colossians 2:12). What Paul is saying in both passages is that in Baptism we *share in the death of Christ* and all the benefits of Christ's death become ours. What are those benefits? The Bible tells us that through His death Jesus has atoned for sin. When we were baptized, we received the forgiveness of all our sins because we have been baptized *into Jesus' death*. The Bible tells us that Jesus' death opened the gates of paradise. When we were baptized, heaven was opened to us because we have been baptized *into Jesus' death*. The Bible tells us that in His death Jesus conquered Satan. When we were baptized, we defeated the devil because we have been baptized *into Jesus' death*. And that's not all. Paul also tells us in these passages that we will be raised to life through our Baptism. This is true because we have been baptized *into Jesus' death* and because in His death Jesus conquered sin, death, and hell. Therefore, nothing has the right to deny us life.

Some people scoff when we attribute such wonderful power to Baptism. They accuse us of being superstitious because we believe that water has such "magical power" to do these things. Apparently, they do not see that it is not the water that does the forgiving and the saving but the Word of

God, which is connected to the water. Baptism is more than pouring water on somebody's head. The water of Baptism is poured in the name of the Father and of the Son and of the Holy Spirit. It is not a small thing to have the name of the only true and all-powerful God combined with the water poured out on one's head in Baptism. When we are baptized into the name of the triune God, we are baptized into the truth of His holy Word. We are baptized into the Christian faith. We are baptized into the church. All these go together. God gives us Himself when He gives us His Word, and the Word creates faith. In this way, the Word also creates the church. We become God's children and heirs of all His promises. All this is the work of Baptism, which is not just water but water connected to the Word of God and applied with His gracious promise.

In view of the marvelous blessings that Baptism brings, I am amazed at how complacent many people are about their Baptism. Everyone over the age of 3 or 4 knows his or her birth date, but do you know the date of your Baptism? It would seem odd if someone said they attached no significance to their birth, but this seems to be exactly the attitude many people take concerning their Baptism. Paul tells us in Titus that when we are baptized, God saves us and the Holy Spirit gives us a new birth and a new life (Titus 3:4–7). This is definitely not insignificant. In his Pentecost sermon, Peter preached: "Repent and be baptized every one of you in the name of Jesus Christ for the forgiveness of your sins, and you will receive the gift of the Holy Spirit. For the promise is for you and for your children" (Acts 2:38–39). This is definitely something important. It is such a comfort to understand the full significance of Baptism: It preserves us in the true faith, calls us to repentance daily, and immerses us in the love of Christ and the forgiveness of sins.

Some of us were baptized as children and some later in life. It makes no difference; the message is the same. Baptism marks us as children of the heavenly Father. In Baptism, we have been buried into the death of Christ so all the benefits of His death become ours. In Baptism, we have risen with Christ to a new life, a spiritual life in which we now live forgiven of all our sins. In our new life, we glorify God because we live our life in repentance. This is precious water, this water of Baptism. It is water empowered by the Word of God. Thus it is a water of life, a water that empowers us to be God's children. If we doubt that Baptism can bring such a blessing, all we need to do is remember the Father's proclamation from heaven: "This is My beloved Son, with whom I am well pleased" (Matthew 3:17). Will God look on us, who have been baptized in His beloved Son, any less favorably?

Baptism marks us as children of the heavenly Father.

When the baptized children of God hear or read the account of Jesus' baptism, they know that it is also about their Baptism. As we see Jesus walking up out of the water, we see ourselves walking with Him. As we hear the voice of the Father, we hear God saying, "You are My beloved child, with whom I am well pleased." As we see the Holy Spirit descending on Jesus in the form of a dove, we see the Spirit descending on us because we have been baptized into the name and into the death of Jesus. Every time we see a Baptism in church, we can rejoice for the person who is being baptized. That infant, child, or adult is receiving all the wonderful blessings God gives in this precious Sacrament. We also should remember our own Baptism daily. As we do so, we are reminded that we have been baptized into fellowship with the triune God. We have been baptized into the family of the saints, into fellowship with the angels. We have been baptized into the faith—into the teachings of the Scriptures, into the creeds, into the church that is one in heaven and on earth.

Jesus tells us to baptize in the name of the Father and of the Son and of the Holy Spirit (Matthew 28:19). The word *baptize* means "to wash with water." But how is the water to be applied? Should the person be immersed? Can the water be sprinkled or poured? Holy Scripture does not answer this question. The method of application is not important because it is the Word of God that makes the Baptism what it is and accomplishes all that Baptism does. It is not water that has the power to forgive sin, to impart the Holy Spirit, and to save—it is the Word of God that has this power.

Our Lord wants us clean, and in Baptism, He cleans us. It is not the water that does the actual cleaning, "but the word of God in and with the water does these things, along with the faith which trusts this word of God in the water," as Martin Luther says in his Small Catechism. "For without God's word the water is plain water and no Baptism. But with the word of God it is a Baptism, that is, a life-giving water, rich in grace, and a washing of the new birth in the Holy Spirit."[1] Baptism cleans us not because the water is applied in a particular way but because the water comes with God's Word. After all, sin cannot be washed away with mere water. The water must be combined with God's Word, which washes away the sin.

Remember the mother and father at the beginning of this chapter? Amid such excruciating pain and sorrow, these parents clung to the promises of God in Baptism. When faced with the death of their daughter, God brought comfort and peace in the glorious promise of the resurrection. Although only weeks old, this little girl died with Christ and rose with Christ in her Baptism. When the time came, she moved from being numbered with the saints on earth to communing with the saints in heaven. Baptism brought comfort not only to the child but also to her parents.

THE LORD'S SUPPER

Late one evening, I received a phone call informing me that one of my members who had been in the hospital for a number of weeks had been moved into the intensive care unit. Thelma was asking that I come immediately to bring her the Lord's Supper. When I arrived, the doctor told me that Thelma was not allowed to have Communion because she was no longer able to keep anything down. "Can't you have a service for her without Communion?" the doctor requested.

Tears rolling down her cheeks, Thelma looked at the doctor. She didn't say a word, but the doctor understood. He consented and allowed me to give her the Lord's Supper. I conducted the service and as her strength allowed, Thelma recited the liturgy with me. I gave her a piece of bread far smaller than my smallest fingernail and three or four drops of wine. I prayed with Thelma and ended the service. Now the tears she was shedding were ones of joy.

Why did this woman so intensely desire to receive the Lord's Supper? Why would any person consider an apparently insignificant meal to be so precious? Why do millions of Christians each week come to the altar with joyful hearts as if they are partaking in a banquet rather than receiving a sip of wine and a wafer of bread? The answer to these questions is simple:

---

*In the Lord's Supper,
we Christians receive our inheritance.*

In this Sacrament, the Lord Jesus gives us His body and His blood for the forgiveness of our sins. Luther says in his Small Catechism: "Where there is forgiveness of sins, there is also life and salvation."[2] With His body and blood, Jesus gives to His church every spiritual blessing He came to give. Once again, at the center of the Sacrament is Jesus.

Jesus brings
heaven to earth.

The Lord's Supper is about what God does for us, not what we do for Him. Because we are sinful, we will always be tempted to look for salvation within ourselves—but precisely because we are sinful, we cannot find salvation within ourselves. Such a search returns us to Mount Sinai. But the Lord graciously has given us a wonderful opportunity to be saved and to experience salvation in His Supper. We cannot ascend into heaven and grasp God, but He comes to us in Jesus' incarnation, He who truly was Immanuel—God with us. As true God and man, Jesus laid down His life and saved us through His death and resurrection. Now in the Lord's Supper, He gives us everything His life, death, and resurrection accomplished. He brings heaven to earth.

The Shepherd's voice calls His bride, the church, to gather around this Meal, and the family of God is at peace and is one. As the saints who are gathered on the earth, our faith receives the comfort and mercy that God gives in the Sacrament of the Altar. In this family Meal, the Lord provides the forgiveness and life that we need. In this eating and drinking, our bodies and souls receive hope and strength as we spend a moment in eternity. In this feast, the family of God becomes one with saints who have gone before and saints throughout the world. Why? Because the resurrected body and blood of Jesus bring us the forgiveness of God, which declares us to be His "holy ones" or "saints."

However, if this reception of our Lord's body and blood is only a pious act done by Christians to demonstrate love for God, then forgiveness is taken out of the mouths of the saints and the Supper becomes simply another law to obey. What is intended to be a gift from the Savior becomes a lonely moment at the fiery foot of Mount Sinai. Such a perspective is the result of not accepting the words of Jesus, who gave this Sacrament. Instead, people rely on their own wisdom to understand this Meal. Thus they fail to see that this Sacrament, too, has its focus on Jesus and His love for us, not our piety and love for Him. We do not give to God in this Meal; instead, God gives to us. Such misunderstandings often result from the abuse of one word: *is.*

Many people and even entire church bodies embrace a contradictory understanding of the simple words Jesus used when He instituted His Supper. Jesus says about the bread: "Take, eat; this is My body" (Matthew 26:26; compare with Mark 14:22). In Luke's Gospel, Jesus' statement is followed

A wondrous miracle occurs when we receive the Lord's Supper.

by the phrase "which is given for you" (Luke 22:19). Subsequent to his conversion, the apostle Paul also received directly from Jesus an account of the institution of the Lord's Supper. In Paul's account, Jesus says, "This is My body which is for you" (1 Corinthians 11:24). In every account, Jesus uses precisely the same words to describe the bread that He distributes to His disciples: "This is My body." Therefore, it is beyond dispute that on the night He was betrayed, Jesus took bread, broke it, gave it to His disciples, and said, "This is My body." And the words Jesus used regarding the cup and what it gives us are equally clear. In Matthew, Jesus says, "This is My blood of the new testament" (Matthew 26:28 KJV). In St. Mark's Gospel, Jesus uses the same words. However, because it is difficult to believe that a wondrous miracle occurs when we receive the Lord's Supper, many have trouble believing Jesus' words. According to our common sense, it is irrational to believe that bread can actually be the body of Jesus. Therefore, Jesus must have meant something else when He said, "This is My body."

Huldrych Zwingli (1484–1531), a contemporary of Luther, tried to convince people that *is* does not mean *is*. Luther had little patience with such a frivolous view. As a result of Zwingli's erroneous beliefs and confession, Luther could not offer the hand of fellowship to Zwingli and his followers. Another common argument against the biblical view of the Lord's Supper is that the Supper is a matter of personal interpretation. Christians, however, know it is a matter of Christ's teachings and our calling to be faithful and to "observe" everything our Lord gave to us (Matthew 28:20). St. Peter teaches: "No prophecy of Scripture comes from someone's own interpretation" (2 Peter 1:20). In other words, every passage of Scripture has only one intended sense. No individual has the right to give God's Word an interpretation contrary to that which God Himself intended. When people propose that the Lord's Supper may be interpreted in many ways, they unknowingly fall into something called rationalism, a system in which the person and personal reason rule the meaning. A person's reason will try to explain away what it cannot understand. Thus rationalism produces thoughts such as "It really doesn't matter what you believe—it's all the same"; "It's only what is in your heart that counts, so it doesn't matter where you commune"; or "Communion is only between me and God, therefore no one can tell me what it means." These thoughts turn God's truth—including the eternal mystery of the real presence of the body and blood of Jesus in the Sacrament—into a relative set of beliefs that may change to fit one's circumstances. It is important that Lutherans, like other Christians, resist this rationalistic approach to Jesus' words. As faithful Christians, we can believe what Jesus said. His words are clear and are not open to interpretation.

The consequence of not believing the Savior's words is tragic. More than just the body and blood of Jesus, this Sacrament is all about our Savior and what He taught. When one denies the real bodily presence, one also denies to oneself the magnificent benefits that God gives in the Sacrament. After all, Jesus offered His body to death by crucifixion and shed His blood on the cross to bring us forgiveness for all our sins. Jesus saved us by destroying death, rising to life, and opening to us the gates of heaven.

Of course, many of those who deny the real presence of Jesus' body and blood in the Lord's Supper do believe that He died to bring us forgiveness and to save us. However, it is sad that they deny the grace Jesus gives in His Supper as they transform it from a gift of grace to an act of obedience. One would think that Ten Commandments were enough, yet once again, people replace grace with works, the Gospel with the Law, and Mount Calvary with Mount Sinai.

Because of its importance, it is worth understanding the Lord's Supper through another scriptural image. Consider again the mountains of Sinai and Calvary. The message that thunders from Sinai is one of God's wrath against those who break His commandments. The Lord declares, "The soul who sins shall die" (Ezekiel 18:4). The Old Testament writers frequently expressed this truth in the phrase "the cup of God's wrath." The cup represented the limits of

God's patience, so to speak. The sins of the people made God angry. His wrath against those people and their sins filled the cup. When the cup was full, the people who had filled it were required to drink from it. What a portrait of the fact that the sinner must be punished, the soul that sins shall die. Consider the following passages and note that drinking the cup of wrath always refers to the unrepentant sinner.

> Let their own eyes see their destruction, and let them drink of the wrath of the Almighty. (Job 21:20)

> For in the hand of the LORD there is a cup with foaming wine, well mixed, and He pours out from it, and all the wicked of the earth shall drain it down to the dregs. (Psalm 75:8)

> Wake yourself, wake yourself, stand up, O Jerusalem, you who have drunk from the hand of the LORD the cup of His wrath, who have drunk to the dregs the bowl, the cup of staggering. (Isaiah 51:17)

> Thus the LORD, the God of Israel said to me: "Take from My hand this cup of the wine of wrath, and make all the nations to whom I send you drink it. They shall drink and stagger and be crazed because of the sword that I am sending among them." (Jeremiah 25:15–16)

This Old Testament cup of God's wrath is a terrible cup, one poured out for those who do not keep God's commandments. Those who drink of it have touched Mount Sinai apart from Jesus and can expect nothing but to drink from the cup of wrath.

But Jesus institutes a New Testament cup—a cup of salvation. First, Jesus, our substitute, drinks the wrathful cup of death that we filled with our sins and rebellion against God. He does not look forward to drinking it. In fact, Jesus prays in the Garden of Gethsemane: "My Father, if it be possible, let this cup pass from Me; nevertheless, not as I will but as You will" (Matthew 26:39). And the Father willed that His Son drink the cup because the Father loves us and knows that we cannot drink the cup and survive. So the Father sends His only Son to drink it for us. And the Son drank every drop, completely consuming the wrath of God. The cup that Jesus drank was a bitter, horrible, eternal cup. No wonder He cried from the cross: "My God, My God, why have You forsaken Me?" (Matthew 27:46).

Having drunk this awful cup for us, Jesus gives us a new cup to drink, a cup of blessing that is filled with forgiveness and grace, love and life. Jesus' passion and His drinking of the cup of wrath are immersed in the gracious cup of the New Testament. After all, what is the significance of Jesus' institution of the new testament of His body and blood? The chalice is not to be feared. Jesus stood under the Law for all people so they may drink the cup of grace. "Drink ye all of it," Jesus says, "for this is My blood of the new testament, which is shed for many for the remission of sins" (Matthew

26:27–28 KJV). We drink from this cup every time we attend the Lord's Supper—and we live.

The cup of wrath has been replaced with the cup of salvation.

So the Lord's Supper is the new testament of Jesus, an inheritance of forgiveness. The true "altar call" is the one in which Jesus calls us to drink from the cup of salvation. Thus in this Sacrament, Jesus says, "Come. Receive. Eat, drink, live, be forgiven. My new testament is one of grace alone." The Lord's "altar call" is different from the popular notion lived out on television because the best many television preachers offer is the demand for an act of piety, which is an act of Law. The majority of television preachers only call believers to "Come. Obey. Remember. Give. Decide. Accept." They view Jesus' *new* testament as possessing the same character as the old covenant of Moses; they see it as Law. Concerning the Lord's Supper, they would seem to be saying that the Law was given through Moses, and Jesus brought the Law again.[3]

Christians are sinners and saints at the same time. The old and new Adam coexist in us. Faith in Jesus is our only hope. We need grace and forgiveness, not new precepts and laws. In the Sacrament of the Altar, Jesus gives us pure Gospel without Law. It is a cup filled with grace and forgiveness, one that can never be emptied. No matter how much we drink, it remains full. God's mercy and forgiveness never come to an end. No matter how often we fail Him and break His Law, God always stands ready to forgive. King David knew of such mercy and in Psalm 23 he demonstrates that though he had not seen the institution of Jesus' cup of mercy in the Lord's Supper, he truly understood the concept: "My cup overflows. Surely goodness and mercy shall follow me all the days of my life, and I shall dwell in the house of the LORD forever" (Psalm 23:5–6).

My appreciation for what Jesus gives us in the Lord's Supper has grown throughout the past three decades. Much of this growth is the result of 20 years spent serving four different congregations. Month after month, year after year, it was my duty and privilege to consecrate bread and wine and to distribute the Savior's body and blood for the forgiveness of sins. I fully understand that when people engage in the same act week after week, it may become routine and tedious. On the other hand, sometimes people can be led to reflect more deeply on such an act and realize anew why it is so special. When I graduated from the seminary in 1975, I believed everything the Bible teaches about the Lord's Supper. My convictions regarding Holy Communion have never changed, but my appreciation for what happens when we receive the Lord's Supper has grown profoundly. The more we realize that it is an eternal feast that feeds and sustains the soul, the more often we will leave the Lord's Table with the deepest awe and rejoicing.

Consider what happens when we receive Holy Communion. When the pastor gives us the bread and we eat it, we receive the body of Jesus. We receive the body of the Son of God, the Son of the Virgin Mary, the Second Person of the Holy Trinity. The mystery of the incarnation is beyond our ability to understand. We confess in faith that "for us men and for our salvation [Jesus] came down from heaven and was incarnate by the Holy Spirit of the virgin Mary and was made man."[4] But who can understand how such a wonder can occur—that God the Son would unite Himself with our human flesh for all eternity? And in this Meal, we participate in another wonder: We receive the body of Jesus; we eat the body of Him who is not only man but also eternal God. We cannot separate Jesus the man from Jesus our God. They are one person.

Therefore, the Lord's Supper is an affirmation of the incarnation of the Son of God. As we receive Jesus' body and blood, we confess our belief in the incarnation. Every time we receive the Lord's Supper, we confess what the apostle John proclaims in the first chapter of his Gospel: "The Word became flesh and dwelt among us" (John 1:14). Every time we receive the Lord's Supper, we celebrate Christmas. Every time we receive the Lord's Supper, we say *amen* to the angel's announcement: "Unto you is born this day in the city of David a Savior, who is Christ the Lord" (Luke 2:11). Every time we receive the Lord's Supper, we eat the true body of Him who was gently carried in the arms of Mary, who was wrapped in swaddling clothes and laid in a manger. Thus in our eating and drinking, we confess that God the Son became a man to save us, and every celebration of Holy Communion is a celebration of Christmas. As children of God, we are excited and joyful to receive the eternal gifts of this Meal. Unlike Christmas presents, this Supper has no batteries to die, parts to break, or sleeves to outgrow.

But it is easy to rob Jesus of His incarnation. John Calvin (1509–1564), another contemporary of Luther, denied the real presence because he taught that though we receive Jesus' body and blood in the Lord's Supper, we do not receive it with our mouths. Rather, Calvin said that in the Lord's Supper faith ascends to heaven where Jesus' body is now confined. There faith feeds on Jesus' body and blood. Unfortunately, Calvin ignored the scriptural teaching that reconciliation between God and man never occurs because we ascend to God but always and only because God descends to us. Calvin's position asks people to do what sinful people have never been able to do: Ascend into heaven and grasp God there. To be saved, God must come to us, which He does in the incarnation. Therefore, Jesus with His body and blood is the one at the center of the Sacrament. It is not about our piety, our love, our dedication, or our commitment. It is about Jesus and His love, His dedication, and His commitment to us.

Lutherans believe that the Lord's Supper saves souls, which is what Scripture teaches. The Supper not only expresses God's desire to save or even the fact that He has saved, but as a means of grace, the Sacrament of the Altar actually does save. How fitting that, in a Sacrament that saves, God would again come to us, not ask us to come to Him. Christ bestows His body and blood, which He has placed in, with, and under the Sacrament. With His body and blood, Jesus imparts to us that which He was sacrificed to bring, namely, forgiveness and life. Thus in the Sacrament God bestows salvation. Faith does not accomplish what happens in the Sacrament; faith simply receives what is offered. Faith has no merit of its own; its merit lies in that which it receives. Faith takes no credit; faith only receives credit.

In the Sacrament God bestows salvation.

Although the incarnation of our Lord is a focus of the Lord's Supper, the primary focus in this Meal is Jesus' death. The incarnation of Jesus did not occur for its own sake. Jesus did not become a man simply to be a man. Rather, the incarnation and everything else Jesus did occurred so He might bring us forgiveness, justify us in God's eyes, and save us. Just as the fact that we become righteous before God for the sake of Jesus' suffering, death, and resurrection must remain at the center of the church's teaching, so also this truth regarding our justification must remain at the center of our celebration of the Lord's Supper. If we were to move into the presence of

God without His declared forgiveness that makes us holy, His presence would kill us. In other words, if considered to be simply an act of piety or obedience that we are required to perform, the Lord's Supper would be turned into the lethal law of Sinai. The holiness that justification brings to us is at the center of the Bible's teaching on the Lord's Supper.

Apart from Jesus' life, death, and resurrection, the presence of His body and blood in the Lord's Supper become another form of mysticism. The Bible does not teach that we only need to be in God's presence. In fact, God's presence is not enough to save us. After all, even nonbelievers grasp the presence of God (see Romans 1). The Lord's Supper is an eternal treasure because our Lord married into one act His life, death, and resurrection. The Lord's Supper brings Jesus to us for our salvation. When we enjoy the real presence of the body and blood of Jesus in the Lord's Supper, we do so because it brings forgiveness.[5]

When Jesus was transfigured before Peter, James, and John, we are told that Jesus, Moses, and Elijah "spoke of [Jesus'] departure, which he was about to accomplish at Jerusalem" (Luke 9:31). Later, we read: "When the days drew near for [Jesus] to be taken up, He set His face to go to Jerusalem" (Luke 9:51). Jesus was determined to go to Jerusalem because there He would finish drinking the cup of God's wrath on our behalf. There our salvation would be completed. Matthew expresses this same determination: "From that time Jesus began to show His disciples that He must go to Jerusalem and suffer many things from the elders and chief priests and scribes, and be killed, and on the third day be raised" (Matthew 16:21). It is toward Jerusalem that Jesus has been living. Therefore, it is toward Jerusalem that Jesus now begins to walk. It is in Jerusalem that Mount Calvary awaits Him, and it is in Jerusalem that our salvation will be completed.

For this reason, Satan tries to keep Jesus from entering Jerusalem. No sooner does Jesus tell His disciples that He must go to Jerusalem to suffer and die than Peter takes Jesus aside and tries to dissuade Him. How does Jesus respond to Peter's attempt to keep Him from Jerusalem? "Get behind Me, Satan! You are a hindrance to Me. For you are not setting your mind on the things of God, but on the things of man" (Matthew 16:23). Through Peter, Satan tries to thwart God's plan of salvation for us by keeping Jesus from Jerusalem where He will sacrifice Himself for the sins of the world.

It is no coincidence that the Gospels devote so much space to the short span of time involved in Jesus' passion and death. All the Old Testament prophecies looked forward to these events. On Calvary, God's promise to the serpent that Eve's offspring would crush the serpent's head was fulfilled (Genesis 3:15). On Calvary, all the beautiful promises in Isaiah 53 were fulfilled. On Calvary, Jesus bore our griefs and carried our sorrows, was wounded for our transgressions, was bruised for our iniquities. Thus when Jesus said to His disciples, "This is My body, which is given for you. Do this in remembrance of Me" (Luke 22:19), it was His intention that the most vivid memory in future observances of the Lord's Supper should be of that event in which His body was sacrificed for the forgiveness of sins.

I visited Helen regularly in the retirement home. She had Alzheimer's disease, so every time I visited, she would ask who I was. Patiently I would answer that I was her pastor. Her inevitable response was "Ach, gratuliere!" ("Oh, congratulations!") Helen lived pretty much in the past, but when Helen and I celebrated the Lord's Supper, it was almost as if someone flipped a switch. She recited the confession of sins, the creed, the Lord's Prayer, and other parts of the service word for word. With great reverence, Helen received the body and blood of Jesus, and there was no doubt that she appreciated the fact that in this Sacrament our Lord showered her with the gifts of forgiveness and life. A beautiful and poignant irony was portrayed in my visits with Helen. Here was a Christian woman whose remembering was all mixed up, yet her Lord remembered her. He fed her faith with His body and blood, and she loved and thanked Him for it. Eventually, the day came when remembering was a thing of the past for Helen. Communing Helen was also a part of her past when she could no longer confess. She couldn't even remember how to speak the name of Jesus. But the Christian faith is not based on what we remember. For Helen, the comfort and hope was in the promise that Jesus remembered her, even when she could no longer remember or confess the name of Jesus.

Anyone who has experienced the suffering and pain of Alzheimer's disease can begin to grasp the importance of remembering in the Lord's Supper. Jesus did not give us this Meal only so we could remember Him; the Lord's Supper does far more than remind us of what He did. It is a family meal in which our Father gives us food to eat. It actually places into our mouths the crucified body of Jesus and His blood, which was shed for the remission of our sins. Along with His body and blood, the Lord's Supper gives all the blessings that Jesus' suffering and death procured for us. Luther clarifies these blessings for us: "In the Sacrament forgiveness of sins, life, and salvation are given us through these words. For where there is forgiveness of sins, there is also life and salvation."[6] Thus when we participate in the Lord's Supper, we participate in the suffering and death of Christ. Jesus places into our mouths everything that His death achieved for us.

Forgiveness, life, and salvation are our inheritance.

There is a beautiful parallel between the picture of Baptism that Paul paints for us in Romans and the experience we have as communicants at the Lord's Table. Paul writes: "Do you not know that all of us who have been baptized into Christ Jesus were baptized into His death? We were buried therefore with Him by baptism into death, in order that just as Christ was raised from the dead by the glory of the Father, we too might walk in newness of life" (Romans 6:3–4). The same thing happens in the Lord's Supper. Just as Jesus died, was buried, and rose again to life, we, who partake of His body, through faith in Him see ourselves dead, buried, yet risen again to a new life of forgiveness under His grace. Our reception of Jesus' body and blood is much more than a memory; it is an actual participation in Jesus' suffering, death, and resurrection for us. When we have communed, it is as if we ourselves had suffered for our sins, died for them, and risen from death to life.

When Helen finally left this earth, I could confidently proclaim to her family and friends that she was in heaven. Even as I preached at her funeral service, Helen enjoyed the eternal feast of everlasting life because she participated in the Eternal Feast here on earth. Her "testimony" was her participation in the teachings, work, and salvation of Jesus in the Lord's Supper. It was a mark of her faith in Christ. Helen trusted in God's promise that Jesus remembered her, even if she could not remember Him. Helen was declared holy and forgiven, even as she suffered under the cross of Alzheimer's disease. Helen's Baptism, weekly confession of faith, and participation in the Lord's Supper offered the earthly testimony that Jesus remembered her.

Those people who believe the Lord's Supper is only something they "should remember" have turned this Meal into another law that does nothing for the soul. Without the work of Jesus in this Sacrament, it becomes a meal that starves the soul and creates despair. No one can remember enough to enter heaven. But God promised never to leave us (Matthew 28:20). Jesus remembered Helen because her name was written in the Book of Life. Jesus remembered Helen because He called her regularly to His Supper and fed her. Jesus remembered Helen because He loved her and died for her. Jesus does the important remembering, even in the Sacrament of the Altar.

When the Lord calls us to eat, we heed that call with thanksgiving and with joy because we know this Meal joins us with all those who have gone before us in the faith. In the Supper, the resurrected Lamb brings heaven to us in His body and blood. God calls and gathers those whom He declares to be holy because they have been washed in the blood of the Lamb. This is why the pastor closes the Proper Preface prior to Communion with these words: "Therefore with angels and archangels and with all the company of heaven we laud and magnify your glorious name, evermore praising you and saying: Holy, Holy Holy Lord, God of Sabaoth. Heaven and earth are full of your glory."[7]

Participation in the Lord's Supper is more than eating a bit of bread and drinking some wine to show our love for Jesus. It is an intensely meaningful participation in Jesus' death and resurrection. Just as we are taught in the Great Commission (Matthew 28:19–20), participation in the church of Jesus is also about His teachings. To participate in this Sacrament is to participate in the Christian confession of faith. The following are some of the central teachings of the Christian faith that can be located in our reception of the Lord's Supper.

- The doctrine of the two natures of Christ in the one person Jesus. Whose body do we receive? That of a man who is God.
- The doctrine of the Trinity. Whose body do we receive? That of a man who is the Second Person of the Trinity.
- The doctrine of the real presence. We receive more than a symbol of Jesus' body or a spiritual Jesus; we receive His body crucified on the cross and His blood poured out for us.
- The doctrine of the incarnation. To confess belief in the real presence in the Lord's Supper is to affirm the doctrine of the incarnation (God the Son became man in Jesus).
- The doctrine of Jesus' substitutionary suffering and death for the sins of the world. In our reception of the Lord's Supper, all that Jesus accomplished for us through His suffering and death becomes ours.
- The doctrine of the resurrection. As we partake of the body of Christ who has risen from the dead and as we are united with Him through the reception of His body, we confess our belief that we, too, will rise. Indeed, in the reception of Christ's risen body, we receive in faith a foretaste of our own resurrection.
- The doctrine of the ascension. As we partake of the body of Jesus that has ascended into heaven, we confess that He intends to bring us to heaven where He is now.

- The doctrine of the church. Through the common reception of Christ's body and blood, we become one body with Him who is the head of the church. Together, we who are the body of Christ become participants in His death and resurrection.
- The doctrine of justification. We don't only obey a command, we participate in much more. The body and blood of Jesus brings forgiveness and life.

Because the Lord's Supper involves so many teachings about Jesus, the church wisely heeds the Lord's wisdom to teach all those who participate. As a parish pastor, I often told people that if these are the teachings about Jesus in which you believe, then you belong at the altar, but even the disciples did not commune until Jesus instructed them, which took three years. St. Paul echoes the Great Commission in his first letter to the Corinthians, "Let a person examine himself, then, and so eat of the bread and drink of the cup. For anyone who eats and drinks without discerning the body eats and drinks judgment on himself" (1 Corinthians 11:28–29). Here, St. Paul acknowledges the importance of the teachings that Christ referred to in the Great Commission. This is why in churches that confess the sacraments as Christ gave them, baptized children and adults commune after a course of instruction that ensures communicants are able to examine themselves as Paul advises.

This practice of communing individuals only after proper instruction leads directly to the Lutheran practice of close(d) Communion. On many Sunday mornings, it was emotionally difficult for me to inform visitors to my congregation that they should wait for instruction before they commune. If the visitors were not Lutheran, then how could I know what they believe? Even if they belonged to another Lutheran denomination, they may not adhere to the teachings of the Lutheran Confessions. This is tough for a pastor and for congregational leadership. No one wants to be rude. But suppose you invite friends to dinner. While cooking the meal, you pay special attention to the seasonings because you want the food to taste good. Therefore, you use salt. As the feast begins, one of your friends informs you that she has a deadly allergy to salt. If only you had known about this while preparing the food. If only you had told your guests about the seasonings before they began to eat.

The Lord's Supper is so much more than a remembrance, a gathering of friends, or an invitation to a dinner. The Lord's Supper is filled with the Gospel of Jesus. What if those gathering at the altar don't believe in Christ? What if they believe the Lord's Supper is only a law? What if they deny that Jesus is present in His flesh and blood? What if they believe that God did not create the world? What if they reject the Trinity? When a pastor teaches the faith to the people, he knows what they believe. They also know what this Supper is all about. This is why believing is more than a matter of the heart, it also involves a public statement of the belief you have in Jesus. The pastor and the congregation are responsible to Christ to proclaim what He taught. The person who communes is responsible for what he or she believes. "So everyone who acknowledges Me before men, I also will acknowledge before My Father who is in heaven" (Matthew 10:32; see also Acts 24:14; Romans 10:9–10; 1 John 4:15).

To allow all those who say they "believe" to participate in the Lord's Supper will open the Sacrament to many who do not know what or in whom they believe. The Christian church has faith in and believes in Jesus. Both pastor and congregation bear the responsibility to ensure that the participants in this Holy Meal believe what Jesus taught.

Participation in the Lord's Supper affirms the unity of the body of Christ. This unity is not expressed if Jesus' body and blood are declared absent. If the real presence of the body and blood of Jesus is denied, all the benefits that the Lord's Supper brings are denied as well. The Lord's Supper ceases to be a celebration of salvation. It ceases to be the gift that God gives to His church. It ceases to be a reception of forgiveness and life. At best, it becomes a corporate, or individual, act of obedience—nothing more than like-minded people getting together to remember what Jesus did. At this point, the Lord's Supper is no longer a distinctively Christian sacrament. The doctrine of the real presence of Christ's body and blood in the Sacrament unites the body of Christ, the church (Ephesians 1:22), in a common confession of faith in the grace of God as it comes to us in the body and blood of the Savior (1 Corinthians 10:16).

Therefore, Lutheran congregations historically invite to

their altars members of those church bodies with whom they share agreement in the teachings of Jesus. This practice accomplishes two things. First, it protects those who don't understand what this Meal offers from the spiritual harm they bring upon themselves if they commune in an unworthy manner. Second, the practice of close(d) Communion preserves what the Lord gave in His Supper. It preserves the Gospel that the Lord gave to His holy family, the church. It is edifying to know that the woman to my left and the man to my right share with me a true unity in Christ's teaching. Not only regarding the Supper are we one, but also in the basic teachings of Christianity. This joyful expression of unity in the faith cannot occur when beliefs are different. Thus the practice of close(d) Communion is not meant to exclude people from God's grace; instead, it is meant to ensure that everyone actually receives the benefit of God's grace when they commune. This practice maintains unity in the faith.

CHAPTER SIX

FONT, PULPIT, AND ALTAR

Zion lives by the
grace God gives.

The Word and Sacraments mark the unity Christians have with one another. In one of his psalms, King David expresses how beautiful unity is:

> Behold, how good and pleasant it is when brothers dwell in unity! It is like precious oil poured on the head, running down on the beard, on the beard of Aaron, running down on the collar of his robes! It is like the dew of Hermon, which falls on the mountains of Zion! For there the LORD has commanded the blessing, life forevermore." (Psalm 133)

David refers to Aaron, not Moses, Zion, not Jerusalem, because he is talking about unity in the church, not in the nation. According to David, unity is good, pleasant, and precious. Where this unity reigns, God's blessing and everlasting life also are present. Recognizing the precious nature of unity, St. Paul stresses to the Ephesians how important it is that they do everything they can to retain it: "[Be] eager to maintain the unity of the Spirit in the bond of peace. There is one body and one Spirit—just as you were called to the one hope that belongs to your call—one Lord, one faith, one baptism, one God and Father of all, who is over all and through all and in all" (Ephesians 4:3–6). Just as God is one, there is also only one body, the church, one Spirit, one faith, one Baptism.

In the Lutheran Church, we attempt to express in our practice this unity extolled by David and Paul. In Lutheran worship, therefore, we recognize the essential unity that exists between the baptismal font, the pulpit, and the altar. The faith into which a child is baptized is the one true faith of which Paul speaks in Ephesians. The faith the pastor proclaims from the pulpit is not his opinion or even his view about the faith. Rather, what he proclaims is the one true faith itself as expressed in the creeds. And the faith confessed at the altar when we receive the Lord's Supper is not the individual faith of each believer. The forgiveness that cleanses you at the Lord's Supper clings to "the faith" of the church. Thus the font, pulpit, and altar express unity of faith. Therefore, Lutheran pastors do not preach from the pulpit anything that differs from that faith into which a child is baptized. Nor do communicants come to the altar with

beliefs and convictions that contradict that which is preached
from the pulpit.

For example, when we are
baptized, we are not baptized
into the name of some god. We
are baptized specifically into the
name of the Father and of the
Son and of the Holy Spirit. The

*God's love
speaks to us
in different
ways.*

preaching of the pastor directs the faith of the people not to
some god but specifically to the triune God. If he does not
preach to lead people to faith in the God of our Baptism, he
is not a faithful preacher. When we attend the Lord's Supper,
we arrive at the altar with those who confess faith in the triune God who places His name on us in Baptism and to
whom the pastor points in his preaching.

To drive any kind of wedge between font and pulpit or
between pulpit and altar—that is, to permit variety or dis-
agreement in the teaching expressed at font, pulpit, and
altar—is to disparage the unity that King David and St. Paul
ask us to treasure. Eventually a practice that does not honor
the essential unity of confession in font, pulpit, and altar will
destroy the church's confession entirely.

When we speak of Baptism, preaching, and the Lord's
Supper, we speak, of course, about life on Mount Zion. We
speak about how the church is born, nourished, sustained,
and preserved to the end. And in each activity, Jesus is at the

center. It is His benefits that are poured with the water on our heads in Baptism. His words are the focus of all preaching. It is His forgiveness and life that we receive together with His body and blood in the Sacrament of the Altar. It is His holy bride with whom He becomes one at the altar.

But there is another kind of unity among font, pulpit, and altar in addition to the unity of confession. Baptism, the preaching of the Gospel, and the Lord's Supper all bring us the same thing—grace. The purpose of Baptism, the Gospel, and the Lord's Supper is the same: to create and preserve faith, faith in Jesus our Savior. This faith is born of, fed, and nourished by only one thing—the grace that comes through Jesus Christ. Thus just as the Israelites were sustained by manna sent from heaven, so Zion lives by the grace God sends from heaven in His Son, Jesus Christ, the grace that comes to us in Baptism, the Gospel, and the Lord's Supper.

Grace is of inestimable value. Without it, we are alienated from God; with it, we are in fellowship with Him. Without it, we are hopeless; with it, we have a living hope and an imperishable inheritance (1 Peter 1:3–4). Without it, we are lost forever; with it, we live forever. It often happens, unfortunately, that sinful people do not know or appreciate the great value of God's grace. As a result, people may question why they need to be baptized, especially if they already believe in Jesus and the forgiveness He won on the cross. These same people may question the need to approach the altar because they already possess what the Lord's Supper gives. Such reasoning may appear to make sense, but it becomes irrational upon closer examination. Yes, Christians who come to faith in Christ as adults, for example, already have complete forgiveness for all their sins. If they die, they will go to heaven. They cannot be "more forgiven" than they are the moment they believe in Jesus. Baptized and believing children of God live constantly under God's grace and are no "less forgiven" on a Saturday night before Communion than on Sunday morning after they have received the Sacrament. Operating with this rationale, a person might decide never to be baptized or never to receive the Lord's Supper.

But operating with this rationale, a person ignores the reason for which the sacraments were given. They are treasures. They are God's grace. They are not obligations placed on us to fulfill. They are gifts. They do not burden faith; they feed faith. What person in his right mind and under normal circumstances would refuse the food he desperately needs to sustain his life? Grace is the food that feeds our faith and sustains it. Why would we refuse it? People who refuse to be baptized or who neglect to come to the Lord's Supper don't believe what the Bible says concerning God's gifts in these sacraments.

Imagine that I own a field full of treasures and I permit you to walk in it. I give you a bag and tell you to keep whatever you find. A few yards into your walk, you find several diamonds, which you place in your bag before continuing your walk. A few yards later, you discover several large rubies. Do you leave them where they are because you already have diamonds? Most of us would be delighted to have diamonds and rubies, so you add the rubies to your bag and continue on. Then you come across some stunning emeralds. What do you do? Diamonds, rubies, and emeralds are all precious jewels. You would not despise the one simply because it did not have the same appearance as the others. Value comes in many different forms. What would you think of a person who said, "My sister inherited a million dollars in gold, but I inherited a million dollars in silver. I am so upset"? Just as gemstones, silver, and gold are different but all connote wealth, so God also has more than one way to show and give His love to us: the Gospel, Baptism, and the Lord's Supper. His love and grace have no less value because they came by a different means. Instead, God uses all three means of grace to assure us that He loves us.

In the proclamation of the Gospel, there is no question about whom God wishes to forgive and save. The Bible says: "The Lord . . . is not willing that any should perish, but that all should come to repentance" (2 Peter 3:9 KJV). In his first letter to Timothy, Paul says that God "desires all people to be saved and to come to the knowledge of the truth" (1 Timothy 2:4). Jesus said: "God so loved the world, that He gave His only Son, that whoever believes in Him should not perish but have eternal life" (John 3:16). And Paul proclaims that "[Christ] died for all" (2 Corinthians 5:15). The Gospel makes clear that God loves everyone; God sent His Son for everyone; Jesus died for everyone. Therefore, we can be confident that Jesus is our Savior. Because of sin, however, we may doubt this fact, so God speaks His love and forgiveness to us in another way. He pours water on our heads and we are baptized into His name. In the same way, God makes it clear in the Lord's Supper that His grace is meant specifically for each person at the altar. We can have no doubts that God's forgiveness is meant for us when the body of the Savior is placed into our mouths. We can have no doubts that Jesus means to save us when He gives us to drink of His own blood shed for us on the cross.

God's love speaks to us in different ways, but it is the same love He speaks whether in the Gospel, Baptism, or the Lord's Supper. His forgiveness, salvation, and life are imparted in a different fashion, but they are the same forgiveness, life, and salvation that Christ earned for us on Mount Calvary and that are imparted to us on Mount Zion. These treasures of God create, nourish, and preserve Zion during her pilgrimage on earth and prepare her for the day she will meet the Savior face-to-face and grace will culminate in everlasting glory.

CHAPTER SEVEN

WE WILL LIVE FOREVER

Christianity contains many mysteries, many paradoxes, and many teachings that are difficult to understand. It is not easy to understand the Trinity—that God could be one single being yet three divine and distinct persons. It is not easy to understand the incarnation—that God the Son could become a baby, lying in the arms of a woman who is His mother. How can Jesus be fully human yet at the same time the eternal God? But the scene that confronts us in Jesus' death is one of the hardest to comprehend. God the omnipotent, God the eternal, God the Son, the Holy One lies buried in a grave.

> O darkest woe! Ye tears forth flow!
> Has earth so sad a wonder?
> God the Father's only Son
> Now is buried yonder.
> O sorrow dread!
> Our God is dead![1]

Why does the Son of God lie in a grave? The Scriptures give a clear answer to this question: Jesus is the Lamb, the great Passover Lamb. When the children of Israel had lived in Egypt for 430 years, God sent His prophet Moses to tell Pharaoh to let the Israelites go. Following a series of plagues meant to cause Pharaoh to release the Israelites from their captivity, Pharaoh remained hard-hearted and refused to release them. So God decided to send His angel to strike dead all the firstborn of the people of Egypt. Meanwhile, God prepared the Israelites for this plague by instructing them to kill a lamb, eat it, and spread its blood on the doorposts and lintels of their homes. Thus the angel of death passed over the homes protected by the blood of a lamb but took the firstborn of all the families of Egypt. Then Pharaoh let the people go, and the Israelites began their exodus from Egypt.

In the person of Jesus a greater lamb has come, a lamb that had to be sacrificed so the greatest Passover of all could occur. This Lamb of God was sacrificed for the sins of the whole world, and now God passes over all our guilt, shame, and every single sin we have ever committed. Countless thousands of lambs were sacrificed in Egypt so the angel of death might pass over the homes of the Israelites, but the value of those sacrifices is of little consequence in comparison to the sacrifice Jesus made on Good Friday. So great have our sins against God been that to cover them all a sacrifice of no less value than the Son of God was needed. That's why the Son of God lay in a grave.

Because God has passed over our guilt and sin, every Christian looks forward to another Passover. Just as the angel of death noted the doorposts sprinkled with the blood of a lamb and passed over them and the believing Israelites lived, so today the angel of death passes over those who through faith are sprinkled with the blood of Jesus. Thus when life on this earth is over, the soul of the believer goes immediately to heaven to be with God. Upon death the souls of Christians enter the Promised Land of heaven immediately because when Jesus died, a far greater Passover Lamb was sacrificed. We now await our own Passover, our own personal exodus from this world of hardship and trouble. Our soul will be with our Lord in Paradise while our body lies in the grave, awaiting the Day of Resurrection and the return of our Lord. One day each of us will meet death, but for those who live in Zion, death gives way to a new and eternal life.

Only God can bring life out of death.

To bring life out of death for all who believe in Him, God sends His Son to conquer death. See the man Jesus, lying dead in His grave, but He is the Son of God and death cannot hold Him. Jesus rises to life, ascends to heaven, sits at the right hand of the Father, rules all things, prepares a place for us, and looks to the day when He will come again as judge of the living and the dead.

Jesus conquers death by raising Himself from death to life. The importance of Jesus' resurrection cannot be overestimated. The Christian faith stands or falls with the resurrection of Jesus. Any faith without the resurrection of Jesus is nonsense. If the one who came to save us from death lies still and cold forever in a grave, Christianity is a sad joke. St. Paul says: "If Christ has not been raised, your faith is futile and you are still in your sins. Then those also who have fallen asleep in Christ have perished. If in this life only we have hoped in Christ, we are of all people most to be pitied" (1 Corinthians 15:17–19). Those who would deny the resurrection of Jesus and who would reduce Christianity to a set of moral principles have little to do with the apostle Paul, who declares: "If you confess with your mouth that Jesus is Lord and believe in your heart that God raised Him from the dead, you will be saved" (Romans 10:9). Paul even said that if Jesus did not rise, he, Paul, was a false witness and a man without hope (1 Corinthians 15:14–15).

Either Jesus rose from the grave or He did not. If He did not, there is little in life that really matters. We can have no hope. We can have no lasting joy. We can have no solid foundation on which to base our faith and our lives. But if Jesus did rise, the future has hope, our lives have meaning, and His Word provides a strong

Jesus' resurrection is a victory for us.

foundation on which to build and by which to live. And Jesus did rise! St. Paul declares: "But in fact Christ has been raised from the dead, the firstfruits of those who have fallen asleep" (1 Corinthians 15:20). Again, in reference to Jesus' resurrection, Paul exclaims: "Thanks be to God, who gives us the victory through our Lord Jesus Christ" (1 Corinthians 15:57). And Jesus' resurrection is a victory for us.

Frequently, it is difficult to believe that our lives contain anything victorious. It is difficult to believe that evil does not triumph over good. It is difficult to believe that Jesus really accomplished anything for us when we see how faithful Christians suffer and our faith seems at times to be futile. Then we look at the passion and death of Jesus. History has known many dark hours but none as black as those hours when the Son of God was on the cross. There the powers of evil converged on Jesus and released their full fury. Who could have believed that any good could have come out of this? But God took this darkest moment and out of it He brought forgiveness, life, and everlasting glory. That is why our faith ultimately can conquer evil in this world—not because nothing will ever go wrong for us and we will never suffer, never sin, and never succumb to temptation, but because the Son of God took on Himself our human flesh and through His suffering, death, and resurrection robbed the devil and his evil forces of all hope for a final victory. In fact, Jesus' resurrection is the declaration that God already has defeated all evil through Christ, His Son. In the resurrection God has passed sentence on Satan and on all the evil that nailed Christ to the cross.

While in the Colorado Rockies, my wife and I were walking some distance behind an older man. Suddenly, we heard a commotion. We rushed to the man and found him beating a rattlesnake with a large stick. Then he sharpened another stick, which he drove through the snake's head. As we made our return trip along the trail about an hour later, we came on the body of that snake. It was still writhing. Satan is like that snake. His head was crushed at Calvary, he has been defeated, and it is only a matter of time before his fight against God and His church comes to an end. The outcome of the struggle between God and Satan is not in doubt. Satan's still writhing, so to speak, but the decisive battle is over. The victory belongs to God and to His children. But many professing Christians seem to share the attitude that the disciples had before they learned of Jesus' resurrection. His followers locked themselves in a room out of fear of those who had killed their leader. Their hopes were dashed, their plans destroyed. The disciples didn't know that any victory had been won, so they lived without hope. Then news came of the resurrection. Christ had been victorious, and they knew that His victory was also their victory.

The Christian faith is grounded in the historical fact of Jesus' resurrection.

Many people still live in that locked room, terrified and hopeless. They need to be told that because Christ is alive, a real victory belongs to them. Jesus says in the Book of Revelation: "Fear not; I am the first and the last, and the living one. I died, and behold I am alive forevermore, and I have the keys of Death and Hades" (Revelation 1:17–18). Because Jesus lives, the final victory over sin, over death, and over hell belongs to every Christian. It is not a losing cause to be a Christian. Our Savior is mighty, and He is able to deliver us from sin and to give us a hope that cannot be destroyed, the hope of our personal victory over death. When believers in Christ approach death, the gates of death will not be able to turn them back. Believers do not go to death as slaves or as prisoners to a dungeon. Rather, they go through death into the presence of their victorious Savior. This is not wishful thinking, the fantasy of miserable people who have created a hope for themselves so they don't have to despair. Our faith is grounded in the historical fact of Jesus' resurrection. Our faith is grounded in the promise of God, who gives victory and salvation to all who believe in Jesus.

Our perspective of something determines our attitude about it. For example, if you are hungry and an apple is in the middle of the table, you may be tempted to take a bite. But change your perspective by walking to the other side of the table, and you see a large rotten spot in the apple. Your mouth stops watering because you certainly are not going to take a bite out of that particular apple. Your attitude toward the apple depended on your perspective. Your perspective can be right, wrong, or incomplete. The reason many people fear death is that their perspective is wrong or incomplete. They operate with an unbeliever's view that death is the end, the snuffing out of human existence, the period that marks the conclusion of a human life after which there is nothing more.

When my oldest son was a young boy, I wanted to teach him not to run out into the street. One day, when no cars were coming, I took him out into the street and showed him a squirrel that had been hit by a car. We agreed that the squirrel was dead, that it would never run again, play again, climb a tree again. My son asked why the squirrel was dead, so I explained that the squirrel had run into the street—right in the path of a car. Unfortunately, many people have drawn theological conclusions from similar experiences. They see animals and people die and they never see anyone or anything live again, so they conclude that when we die, we're done. We'll never run or play again.

But that's not the Christian view of death. We know that the moment Christians die, their souls go immediately to God in heaven. The Book of Ecclesiastes says: "The dust returns to the earth as it was, and the spirit returns to God who gave it" (Ecclesiastes 12:7). St. Paul says: "My desire is to depart and be with Christ, for that is far better" (Philippians 1:23). And the Book of Revelation says: "Blessed are the dead who die in the Lord from now on" (Revelation 14:13). Jesus once told a parable about a rich man and Lazarus, who was poor. Jesus said that when Lazarus died, the angels carried him to Abraham's side (Luke 16:22). Jesus said to the thief on the cross, "Today you will be with Me in Paradise" (Luke 23:43) and to Martha, "I am the resurrection and the life. Whoever believes in Me, though he die, yet shall he live, and everyone who lives and believes in Me shall never die" (John 11:25–26).

Death is not the termination of human existence. Death is not the snuffing out of a human being. In fact, when a Christian dies, the angel of death passes over completely. Although we may place the body in the ground, the soul of that person is in heaven with Jesus and the angels and all the saints.

> Thanks to Thee, O Christ victorious!
> Thanks to Thee, O Lord of life!
> Death hath now no power o'er us,
> Thou hast conquered in the strife.[2]

When Jesus said from the cross that "It is finished," those words meant that His victory had been completed. When He entered death, Jesus did not enter death in defeat. Instead, Jesus subdued and conquered death. His victory is evident when He dies. We're told in the Gospel of Matthew that when Jesus died "the tombs also were opened. And many bodies of the saints who had fallen asleep were raised, and coming out of the tombs after His resurrection they went into the holy city and appeared to many" (Matthew 27:52–53). Look at the victory Jesus brings with His death. The Son of God dies and believers in Him rise because as Matthew tells us, when Jesus died, "the curtain of the temple was torn in two, from top to bottom" (Matthew 27:51). This curtain prevented the people from entering the Holy of Holies, which symbolized the presence of God. Now that the Lamb of God had been sacrificed, the curtain was torn from top to bottom because this Lamb had taken away the sins of the world. Now nothing can separate us from the love of God that is in Christ Jesus our Lord—not even death.

Certainly death cannot separate from the Father the one who has conquered it, namely, Jesus Christ, His only Son. As a conqueror, Jesus walks right through death into heaven, which is what we will do because we believe in Jesus. We are covered with the blood of the Passover Lamb. By the power of Jesus' death and resurrection, we will walk right through death into heaven. Finally, on the last day, when our Lord returns to judge the living and the dead, He will raise our bodies to life again. Then our souls and bodies will be reunited, and we will live forever in the kingdom Jesus has prepared for us from the foundation of the world (Matthew 25:34).

Is heaven "the end" for Christians? We cannot use the word *end* to describe our future because there is no end. Our life with Christ and all the saints and angels is eternal. Jesus says: "God so loved the world, that He gave His only Son, that whoever believes in Him should not perish but have eternal life" (John 3:16). He also says: "My sheep hear My voice, and I know them, and they follow Me. I give them eternal life, and they will never perish, and no one will snatch them out of My hand. My Father, who has given them to Me, is greater than all, and no one is able to snatch them out of the Father's hand" (John 10:27–29). John the Baptist says: "Whoever believes in the Son has eternal life" (John 3:36).

Who can describe how good and kind our God is to His children? Paul reminds us that "no eye has seen, nor ear heard, nor heart of man imagined what God has prepared for those who love Him" (1 Corinthians 2:9). The glory of what God has prepared for us in heaven is beyond description, but we know one thing. Although there is no "end" for Christians, there will be an end to all worries, temptations, and trials, to all crying and pain. Then

> All trials shall be like a dream that is past;
> Forgotten all trouble and mourning.
> All questions and doubts have been answered at last,
> When rises the light of that morning.
>
> The heavens shall ring with an anthem more grand
> Than ever on earth was recorded;
> The blest of the Lord shall receive at his hand
> The crown to the victors awarded.[3]

CHAPTER EIGHT

THE OFFICE OF THE HOLY MINISTRY

W ithout the treasures of God's grace, Zion dies. Without the Gospel, the church cannot survive. Without forgiveness, faith expires. The benefits of Calvary must continue to be dispensed to Zion. Just as our bodies must be fed with good food and drink to remain healthy and alive, so faith, too, must be fed. For this reason, the church historically has met at least weekly to be fed with the Word of God. Jesus' institution of the Lord's Supper also implies frequent reception: "Do this, as often as you drink it" (1 Corinthians 11:25). As the body craves food, the soul of the Christian craves grace and forgiveness.

So the Christian may be fed on a regular basis with the Gospel and the Sacrament, God has instituted the office of the holy ministry. The first uniquely Lutheran confessional document, the Augsburg Confession, talks about how God has created this office for the sake of His people, whose faith cannot survive without the Gospel:

> In order that we may obtain this faith, the ministry of teaching the Gospel and administering the sacraments was instituted. For through the Word and the sacraments, as through instruments, the Holy Spirit is given, and the Holy Spirit produces faith, where and when it pleases God, in those who hear the Gospel. That is to say, it is not on account of our own merits but on account of Christ that God justifies those who believe that they are received into favor for Christ's sake. Gal. 3:14, "That we might receive the promise of the Spirit through faith."[1]

God provides for all His people's needs. The Father sends His Son to earn forgiveness for us. The Father and the Son send the Spirit to cause the apostles to record the news of this wonderful salvation. Then God establishes the office of the ministry so the Word of the prophets and the apostles will continue to be preached to God's people until the Savior returns. Through this office, God causes His church to grow. Through this office, the Gospel will be proclaimed and people will be brought to and sustained in the faith. Therefore, a pastor is primarily a preacher or a proclaimer of God's Word and specifically of God's grace. He is ordained into the ministry to bring to people God's Gospel and the Sacraments. It is his task to distribute the treasures of Zion. The holy ministry is not an office that exists for its own sake. Rather, God calls pastors into service in the church and for the sake of the church.

Conflict and stress are all too common in the relationships between pastors and congregations. Overlooking the fact that the office of pastor is established by God to preach His Word, congregations sometimes release pastors for unscriptural reasons. On the other hand, some pastors act in an authoritarian fashion. A potential corrective for pastors and laypeople who cannot maintain a balanced view of the ministerial office is to consider the meaning of two historic Latin terms that have been used as titles for those who hold the office of preaching God's Word in the congregation. The words are *pastor,* which means "shepherd," and *minister*, which means "servant," but even these words and images need to be held in proper balance. If people focus on the concept of the minister as servant to shape their paradigm of the minister, it may be difficult for the pastor to serve as a shepherd. If the concept of servant takes precedence and the pastor is viewed as an employee, a hired hand, a contracted worker, it may be impossible for the people to hear the pastor's words from the pulpit as the words of God. There may be a strong temptation to get rid of the pastor when his message is no longer pleasing, even if the message is in accord with God's Word. Conversely, if the pastor focuses exclusively on the concept of shepherd, that is, if he forgets or ignores the fact that he is also a servant, he may forget that the office he holds was not intended for the benefit of the one who holds it but for the benefit of the people to whom he ministers. Although the sheep are required to listen to the voice of the one whom God has placed in their midst as shepherd, some pastors seem to think their authority goes beyond that which Scripture gives. They do not take seriously Jesus' example of service (Matthew 20:28).

If laypeople remember, however, that pastors are not only servants but also shepherds commissioned by God to feed them with His Word, and if pastors will remember that they are not only shepherds but also servants of Jesus Christ and of the church to which He sends them, God's people will experience a far more harmonious life together. Undoubtedly, pastors and laypeople will be less likely to abuse the office of the ministry if they remember that it is an office established by God Himself. Martin Luther spoke eloquently and frequently about the office of the holy ministry. On one occasion he wrote:

> I hope, indeed, that believers, those who want to be called Christians, know very well that the spiritual estate [the office of the ministry] has been established and instituted by God, not with gold or silver but with the precious blood and bitter death of his only Son, our Lord Jesus Christ [I Pet. 1:18–19]. . . .

He paid dearly that men might everywhere have this office of preaching, baptizing, loosing, binding, giving the sacrament, comforting, warning, and exhorting with God's word, and whatever else belongs to the pastoral office. . . . Indeed, it is only because of the spiritual estate that the world stands and abides at all; if it were not for this estate, the world would long since have gone down to destruction.[2]

As far as Luther is concerned, the feeding of the flock and the growth of the church (there is no difference between the two) occurs only when the Word is preached. Because God has instituted the pastoral ministry so the flock, which is precious to Christ, may be fed, there is an inseparable relationship between the pastoral ministry and the preaching of God's Word. The relationship is so intimate that the preacher ought to be able to say that it is truly God who speaks to the people through his preaching. Thus the faithful pastor must be able to say, as Luther does, "Whenever you hear me, you hear not me, but Christ. I do not give you my baptism, my body and blood; I do not absolve you. But he that has an office, let him administer that office in such a way that he is certain that it comes from God and does everything according to the Word of God, not according to our free will."[3] Thus God speaks through the pastor, who truly stands in the place of Christ. Because God loves the sheep, Luther says about the pastors: "It is their duty to tend

His sheep and give them pasture. Therefore to give pasture is nothing else than to preach the Gospel, by which souls are fed and made fat and fruitful, and that the sheep are nourished with the Gospel and God's Word. This alone is the office of a bishop."[4]

The pastor's preaching should always be focused on Christ.

As Luther indicates, the connection between the pastor and the Word is more specifically a connection between the pastor and the Gospel. Therefore, the pastor's preaching should always be focused on Christ. The office of the ministry itself is Christocentric, that is, Christ is at its center. Therefore, this office constantly points to Jesus, His person and His work, so faith in the Son of God may be created and the church expanded. The proper work of a pastor is, in the words of Luther, to speak "a word of salvation, a word of grace, a word of comfort, a word of joy, a voice of the bridegroom and the bride, a good word, a word of peace"[5] so the church may rejoice in the knowledge of her salvation. This theme is predominant in Luther's writings throughout his life. Even in one of his earliest writings, "Explanations of the Ninety-five Theses," Luther condemns sermons that are not preached to engender and nourish faith in Jesus. He exclaims: "May every single sermon be forever damned which persuades a person to find security and trust in or through anything whatever except the pure mercy of God, which is Christ."[6]

The office of the ministry is not a Mosaic office. It is not an office meant to bring people to Sinai, to encourage them to live there, to gain their hope there, and to stand before God there. The office of pastor is an office of the Gospel. In fact, we often call them ministers of the Gospel. Paul never said, "Woe to me if I do not preach the Law," but he did exclaim, "Woe to me if I do not preach the gospel!" (1 Corinthians 9:16). This does not mean that pastors should not preach the Law, which they must do if people are to see the futility of living on Sinai and embrace the riches of Calvary so they might live on Zion. The preaching of the Gospel is despised when people do not hear the Law and come to a knowledge of their sin. But the glory of the pastoral ministry is not in preaching God's Law, which condemns. At the center of the pastoral ministry is Christ, who brings grace, forgiveness, salvation, and life. That's why pastors are happy when they baptize someone because the Sacrament of Holy Baptism brings Christ's benefits, namely, salvation. That's why pastors are happy when they distribute Jesus' body and blood to sinners in the Sacrament of the Altar, which brings Christ and His forgiveness to sinners. That's why pastors are happy to preach because though preaching may present the Law, it is primarily the preaching of Christ and Him crucified.

Unfortunately, in many churches preachers do not seem to understand the nature of their own office. Thus the major thrust of their preaching is not on the grace and forgiveness found in the Savior but on the importance of living a good life. This sends hearers back to Sinai! But the office of pastor is not centered on Sinai—it is centered on Christ. Christ is at the center of the Gospel, which brings the message of forgiveness through His suffering and death. Christ is at the center of Baptism because in this sacrament all Christ's benefits are bestowed on those who are baptized into His death. Christ is at the center of the Lord's Supper because His body and blood bring forgiveness of sins and eternal life to all who trust in Him. Christ is at the center of Zion's life because Zion derives its life from Him. Therefore, the office of the ministry is not an office about the pastor, it is an office about Jesus. It is an office created by God to proclaim Jesus as Savior, as the one who bore all the world's sin and guilt that He might bring grace and forgiveness to sinners. For pastors, this means that when they preach about Jesus they are to preach not only that He is the Son of God but also that He is the Son of God who came to forgive. They are to preach not only that He died on a cross but also that He died on a cross for our sins, to forgive us so we could live

> *The office of the ministry is an office about Jesus.*

forever. They are to preach not only that He rose from the dead but also that He rose from the dead for us so we, too, will rise one day as children of grace to inherit a beautiful kingdom.

People need to hear that Jesus brings grace. It is wonderful that people believe the pastor when he preaches about the Trinity, the incarnation, the miracles and teachings of Jesus. It is a good thing that people believe the pastor when he preaches about the two natures in Christ (human and divine) and about the humiliation and exaltation of Jesus according to the human nature. But these teachings will not cause the people to rejoice unless they know what Jesus has done for them. Such rejoicing occurs when the pastor preaches about the forgiveness of sins. The people rejoice when the pastor shows them what Jesus did on Mount Calvary so they might stand before God on Mount Zion, forgiven, cleansed, and holy.

Faithful pastors want people to live, not perish, so they preach the Gospel. They proclaim to people that no matter what they have done, God forgives it. No matter what shame they feel, God washes them clean. No matter what wrongs haunt them and never leave them in peace, Jesus, the Lamb of God, has taken them all away. Pastors proclaim that grace not only covers every sin, grace is universal, which means it covers every sinner. No one can say that Jesus didn't come for me, didn't die for me. St. Paul says: "In Christ God was reconciling the world to Himself, not counting their trespasses against them" (1 Corinthians 5:19). When pastors preach the Gospel in this way, the people of God rejoice because they see Jesus. They see Him not as one rising out of the thunder, lightning, and smoke of Sinai to condemn, accuse, and threaten, but as the crucified one who forgives, saves, and justifies. As Jesus said, "God did not send His Son into the world to condemn the world, but in order that the world might be saved through Him" (John 3:17).

The truth that we are justified by grace through faith in Jesus Christ is the doctrine on which the church stands or falls. It is the central teaching of the Christian faith. This truth should always stand at the center of Christian preaching: God loves us and forgives us for Jesus' sake. Thus when the pastor preaches about Jesus' incarnation, he does so to tell people that Christ Jesus came into the world to save sinners. When the pastor preaches about the death of God the Son, he does so to talk about how Jesus' death is substitutionary. When the pastor preaches about Jesus' resurrection, he does so to remind hearers that Jesus "was delivered up for our trespasses and raised for our justification. Therefore, since we have been justified by faith, we have peace with God through our Lord Jesus Christ. Through Him we have also obtained access by faith into this grace in which we stand, and we rejoice" (Romans 4:25–5:2).

John the Baptist said about Jesus that "He must increase, but I must decrease" (John 3:30). John's sentiment is shared by every Christian pastor who knows his duty. The office of pastor is not about the one who holds the office but about the one who instituted the office. St. Paul held the office, but he says, "I decided to know nothing among you except Jesus Christ and Him crucified" (1 Corinthians 2:2). Pastors spend many years baptizing, instructing children, teaching adults, administering the Lord's Supper, preaching, marrying, burying, comforting, admonishing sinners, visiting the sick, defending the faith, warning against false teachers, advising, encouraging, nourishing, and strengthening. They do this for one purpose: that the flock of Christ may know the Shepherd, that sinners may know the Savior. Like John the Baptist, faithful pastors continuously point people to Jesus and say, "Behold, the Lamb of God, who takes away the sin of the world!" (John 1:29).

C. F. W. Walther, the first president of the Missouri Synod, knew this focus well. Like John the Baptist, Walther pointed unwaveringly to Jesus Christ as the Lamb of God who takes away the sin of the world. In his most well-known work, *The Proper Distinction between Law and Gospel*, Walther constantly points to Jesus as our only hope. Walther expected other preachers to do the same thing. In one of his evening lectures, Walther says:

> Here is the Biblical doctrine: The sinner is to come to Jesus just as he is, even when he has to acknowledge that there is nothing but hatred of God in his heart, and he knows of no refuge to which he may flee for salvation. A genuine preacher of the Gospel

will show such a person how easy his salvation is: Knowing himself a lost and condemned sinner and unable to find the help that he is seeking, he must come to Jesus with his evil heart and his hatred of God and God's Law; and Jesus will receive him as he is. It is His glory that men say of Him: Jesus receives sinners.[7]

In another of his evening lectures, Walther states: "It is a great and awful sin not to draw any soul that has been entrusted to us for instruction to Jesus and not to tell that soul again and again what a treasure it has in the Lord Jesus, its Savior."[8]

This message about Christ, the Lamb of God who took away the sin of the world, is the message the church needs to hear. This message gives birth and life to the church. So Walther preached this message because he loved the church. He expected all faithful pastors to have this same focus on Christ. Only when the pastor exercises his office with Christ at the center can his office be considered holy. The office of pastor is not a holy office because of the one who holds it. Instead, it is holy because it always points to Christ, who is holy. Through the pastoral office comes the proclamation of the holy Gospel that makes holy in the eyes of God all who believe in Christ, the administration of a holy Baptism that washes away the sins of all who receive it, and the distribution of holy body and blood of Christ that brings righteousness and holiness to those who eat and drink in faith.

What an honor God gives to pastors because it truly is

an honor and a blessing to serve God's people. Thankfully, the message does not originate with pastors nor does it depend on pastors. God does not send men out to be pastors and tell them to be imaginative. As Paul says to the Galatians: "I would have you know, brothers, that the gospel that was preached by me is not man's gospel. For I did not receive it from any man, nor was I taught it, but I received it through a revelation of Jesus Christ" (Galatians 1:11–12). And Paul says to the Corinthians:

> And I, when I came to you, brothers, did not come proclaiming to you the testimony of God with lofty speech or wisdom. For I decided to know nothing among you except Jesus Christ and Him crucified. . . . My speech and my message were not in plausible words of wisdom, but in demonstration of the Spirit and of power, that your faith might not rest in the wisdom of men but in the power of God. As it is written, "What no eye has seen, nor ear heard, nor the heart of man imagined, what God has prepared for those who love him"—these things God has revealed to us through the Spirit. (1 Corinthians 2:1–2, 4–5, 9–10).

When pastors and laypeople truly understand the nature of the office of the holy ministry, God is glorified by His people and Zion experiences God's peace.

CHAPTER NINE

ZION SINGS

A few years ago, I was a guest preacher at a midwestern Lutheran congregation. Because of where I was sitting, I could observe the acolyte as he walked down the aisle, lit the candles, and sat down. Observing his tennis shoes and ragged jeans peeking from beneath his robe, I wondered why an acolyte would dress in a manner that didn't show respect for the occasion. As the service began, I noticed the acolyte did not open his hymnal. I wondered if he understood that he was in God's presence, that we were going to listen to God's Word and receive His blessings of forgiveness and life. But when the congregation began to sing the liturgy, I was ashamed of my thoughts. This young boy sang the entire service from memory and with enthusiasm. He joined in every hymn. I had been quick to pass judgment. I may appreciate black shoes and dress slacks, but they will never be a substitute for what I saw that Sunday morning.

That young boy painted a beautiful picture of what happens when Zion sings about Jesus. We sing with the same voice, and we sing the same words because we are members of the same family, the family of God. Historically, the Lutheran Church has been "conservative" in its worship, that is, we have used those forms of worship used throughout the centuries by the Christian church. Lutherans continue to recognize the importance of worship as an activity that expresses and preserves the unity of the body of Christ as people gather to hear God's Word of grace and respond in prayer and praise. When people in the same church body hear the same Scripture lessons, pray the same prayers, confess the same creeds, and sing the same hymns, the people share a commonality in worship. Unity in worship enhances and supports unity in the faith. Our sense of family also is strengthened when we attend services at sister congregations and participate with confidence because the liturgy is familiar. It is not only that we have the same Lord, we actually worship Him with the same words.

But uniformity in worship is not important only for the sake of uniformity. The founders of The Lutheran Church—Missouri Synod spoke firmly about the use of hymnals in congregations because it was important that the worship the people experienced in their churches was pure, that is, that it flowed out of Holy Scripture. The Synod's 1854 Constitution declares as one of the reasons for the formation of a synodical organization "the conservation and promotion of the unity of the pure confession,"[1] which requires "the exclusive use of doctrinally pure church and school books, agendas, hymnbooks, catechisms, textbooks, etc.)."[2] This constitution almost belabors the point by continuing:

> If it is not feasible to replace the present unorthodox hymnbooks with orthodox ones in some congregations, the pastor of such a congregation may become a member of Synod only on the condition that he promises that he will use the unorthodox hymnbook only under public protest and gives assurance that he in all seriousness desires to bring about the introduction of an orthodox one.[3]

Finally, this constitution states that the Synod's business is "watching over the purity and unity of doctrine within the Synod."[4] The founders of our church body were wise. They knew that if worship was impure, the teaching and the faith of the people would likewise become tainted. After all, worship is an expression of what we believe and teach.

When we come into God's presence to worship Him, we do not do so with the attitude that any kind of worship will do. David says in one of his psalms: "The LORD is near to all who call on Him, to all who call on Him in truth" (Psalm 145:18). It is important that our worship be based on

---

*Jesus is at the center
of all Christian worship.*

---

the truth of God's Word. For this reason also, it has been the custom of the church to use those liturgies that God's people over the centuries have found to be consistently faithful to God's Word. A worship service that does not reflect the truth of God's holy Word is no proper worship for the family of God. God's children love Him and are profoundly committed to worshiping Him in ways that please Him. This can only happen when the hymns, prayers, confessions, and sermons used in our worship flow from the teachings of God's Word.

At the center of God's Word is Jesus Christ. Thus Jesus is at the center of all Christian worship. Jesus says, "Apart from Me you can do nothing" (John 15:5) and "No one comes to the Father except through Me" (John 14:6). Therefore, all worship apart from Jesus does not worship the true God because apart from Jesus we cannot know God as a loving, gracious Father who forgives and saves sinners for the sake of His Son who gave Himself for them. We must be on guard that worship does not degenerate into moralistic sermons dominated by Law or songs that make no mention of Jesus' work of salvation. Such worship practices deprive people of the joy of truly Christian worship. In the same way, prayers that do not recognize our need for God's mercy in Jesus are dangerous because people will not look to their Savior, Jesus, in their prayers. When worship does not focus on Jesus, it is impossible for the Holy Spirit to create and sustain true faith in the hearts of the people because the Holy Spirit creates faith only by showing people the Savior, Jesus.

In one congregation I served, it became necessary to hire a woman with no background in Lutheran music as our choir director. She was an excellent pianist and organist and had played a lot of popular Christian music. In view of her lack of acquaintance with the Lutheran Church, I asked to approve the music she intended to use, which she didn't consider a problem. After a few months, she asked why I approved only a third of the choral pieces she submitted. I explained to her that Lutherans look for certain elements, such as the mention of the Trinity so hearers know the song is about the triune God. I also pointed out that I looked for pieces that mentioned Jesus and clearly named Him as true God, the Second Person of the Trinity, the Savior of the world. I expressed the importance of a balance of Law that shows our sin and Gospel that saves us from that sin. My criteria also included lyrics that discussed how Jesus' death took our sins away and His resurrection gave us everlasting life. I also noted that hymns and songs should reflect the importance of the sacramental life of the church. After our conversation, the choir director expressed her full understanding of my criteria. A week later she mentioned that she had been reviewing her music collection. "I was so surprised," she said. "Many of the songs use Jesus' name and praise Him, but none of them talk about who Jesus actually is and they don't talk about what He did."

Obviously, not every verse of every hymn, not every sentence of every prayer, not every paragraph of every sermon must speak specifically about who Jesus is and what Jesus did. However, one of the major purposes of every service in a Christian church ought to be to

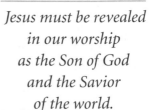

Jesus must be revealed in our worship as the Son of God and the Savior of the world.

show people who Jesus is and what He did for our salvation. It is not enough simply to use His name. He must be revealed in our worship as the Son of God and the Savior of the world. When this does not happen, our worship can no longer be said to be truly Christian.

The worship services or liturgies used in Lutheran churches over the centuries have been truly Christocentric. They are an exquisite proclamation of Law and Gospel and were designed to bring Christ into our presence through the Word. For example, our services begin in the name of the Father and of the Son and of the Holy Spirit. At the center of the divine name is the Son of God—Jesus. In one of our services, when the pastor invites the people to confess their sins, he tells them that they will implore the Father "in the name of our Lord Jesus Christ to grant us forgiveness."[5] During the confession, the people plead for God's mercy "for the sake of the holy, innocent, bitter sufferings and death of your beloved Son, Jesus Christ."[6] The pastor forgives their sins "in the stead and by the command of my Lord Jesus Christ."[7] Then the Kyrie follows in which the congregation sings, "Lord, have mercy; Christ, have mercy; Lord, have mercy."[8] The congregation stands for the reading of the Gospel, which addresses Jesus' birth, life, death, and resurrection. Although it may talk about many things and will certainly present God's Law so people will see their need for a Savior, the sermon's major thrust is the forgiveness, life, and salvation that are ours in Jesus. The central article in the Apostles' and the Nicene Creeds is about Jesus. In many, if not most worship services, the people come forward to receive the body and blood of Jesus, the Lamb of God. And at the service's conclusion, the center of the Benediction is Jesus Christ. Just as the Bible from beginning to end is primarily about Jesus, so the worship service, from beginning to end, is primarily about Jesus.

It is amazing how the Holy Spirit has guided the church over the years to fashion its worship so Christ remains at the center. In fact, if the sermon is poor and does little to edify, the Gospel will still be heard and the Savior will still be "seen" in those churches that use historic liturgies. When the Gospel is heard and the Savior is "seen," then the people's voices will break out in praise from hearts that have been touched by more than sentimental invitations to emotionalism. Instead, the people have been touched by the Holy Spirit, whose joy it is to give life to Zion by showing her Jesus. Then worship becomes not only hearing God's Word and receiving His gifts of forgiveness and life but also our response of gratitude and praise for the one who has called us "out of darkness into His marvelous light" (1 Peter 2:9). Thus our historic worship liturgies unite us, but they do not create a unity that is based on arbitrary forms simply to achieve unity in ritual. Rather, they reflect the unity that all Christians have through their common faith in Jesus Christ. As long as Christ remains the center of worship, our service will be a truly ecumenical event.

Worship can unite us not only with those who surround us on a Sunday morning and with those who worship with the same words we do, it also can unite us with those Christians who have gone before us and with those who will live after us. When we pray and sing with the same words as God's people throughout the centuries, we demonstrate our unity with the church of all time. There are no geographic limits on God's church, nor are there temporal ones. Sometimes when people think about the church, they think only in terms of the present, but membership in the church is not limited to those who are alive. We distinguish between the church militant, that is, those who are still bearing a cross, and the church triumphant, which is those who have laid their crosses down and have gone to live with the Lord. But these are two branches of the same church. The saints in heaven and those of us on earth all stand on Mount Zion together.

In John's Gospel, Jesus says, "I am the vine; you are the branches" (John 15:5). He points out how those branches that do not abide in Him are cut off and cast into the fire to be burned, while the branches that abide in Him, that is, the believers, are never cut off. They remain branches of the true vine, whether they are alive or have gone to heaven. In the Nicene Creed, we confess our belief in "one holy Christian and apostolic Church." Notice, we believe in one church, not two. We are members of the same church as those believers who now live with their Savior and the angels. In the Apostles' Creed, we state that we believe in "the holy Christian Church, the communion of saints," which is the fellowship of the faithful—all the faithful. God's children here and above are in fellowship with one another; we are one family. Thus in its final verse, one well-known hymn describes the church as follows:

> Yet she on earth has union
> With God, the Three in One,
> And mystic sweet communion
> *With those whose rest is won.*
> O blessed heav'nly chorus!
> Lord, save us by your grace
> That we, like saints before us,
> May see you face to face.[9]

We are one family with all God's children down through the ages, and we share an inheritance in our worship with those who have gone before us. We sing the same song as the 144,000 (a figurative statement in Revelation about the number of believers) who even at this moment stand around the throne of the Lamb. Isn't that what we confess each time we receive the Lord's Supper and the pastor prays: "Therefore with angels and archangels and with all the company of heaven we laud and magnify your glorious name, evermore praising you and saying, 'Holy, holy, holy Lord, God of Sabaoth. Heav'n and earth are full of your glory'"?[10] Our voices are joined together with those of the saints and angels in heaven. As one church, one choir, we sing the praises of the Lamb.

We may or may not share the same bloodlines with those who went before, but we do share the same convictions. We confess the same triune God. We look forward with the same hope. We even speak with the same voice. When the pastor opens the service in the name of the Father and of the Son and of the Holy Spirit, we hear the same words that have been heard by members of the church universal since the time of Jesus. By them, we confess our faith in the same gracious Father and confess our fellowship with the baptized of every age because it is into the name of this triune God that we all have been baptized. When we confess our sins, we declare ourselves brothers and sisters of King David, who declared, "I said, 'I will confess my transgressions to the LORD,' and You forgave the iniquity of my sin" (Psalm 32:5). We also identify with the tax collector in Jesus' parable who in great humility confessed, "God, be merciful to me, the sinner!" (Luke 18:13). When we sing the Kyrie, we embrace blind Bartimaeus, who sat outside the gates of Jerusalem and cried out, "Jesus, Son of David, have mercy on me!" (Mark 10:47). When we sing the Gloria in Excelsis or the Hymn of Praise, we join the Christmas angels in praising God for the Savior's birth (Luke 2:14) and John the Baptist in pointing to Jesus as the Lamb of God who takes away the sin of the world (John 1:29). When we speak the words of the Apostles' or Nicene Creed, we confess with our mouths precisely the same convictions the church of Jesus Christ has been expressing for almost two thousand years. Every Christian since the time of Jesus has used the same words to pray the Lord's Prayer. And most worship services conclude with the pastor announcing the same Benediction given to Aaron and used among God's people for more than three thousand years. Thus when we hear "The LORD bless you and keep you; the LORD make His face to shine upon you and be gracious to you; the LORD lift up His countenance upon you and give you peace" (Numbers 6:24–26), we realize again that the faith that lived in the hearts of Moses, Aaron, and the children of Israel is the same faith God has given to us and to all believers. This includes parents who have died in the faith, as well as our children. The holy body of Christ speaks the one language of faith because there is one body, one hope, one Lord, one faith, one Baptism (Ephesians 4:4–5).

Finally, during each Lutheran worship service, appointed Scripture readings are read. These Scripture readings belong to all believers. Shortly before he concludes his Gospel, the apostle John writes: "These [things] are written so that you may believe that Jesus is the Christ, the Son of God, and that by believing you may have life in His name" (John 20:31). John writes for all people who will ever read his message, including us, not only for the Jews of his time. Jesus says as much in His High Priestly Prayer, which He prays to His Father the night of His betrayal. In reference to His disciples, Jesus prays: "I do not ask for these only, but also for those who will believe in Me *through their word*, that they all may be one, just as You, Father, are in Me, and I in You, that they also may be in Us, so that the world may know that You sent Me" (John 17:20–21). All of us who have believed in Jesus through the revelation of the Holy Spirit in the words of the prophets and the apostles are one. And these are our Scriptures; they are about our brothers and sisters in the faith, the people of Zion.

We sometimes forget what it means that all of us who believe in the Savior are members of the same family and that the stories in the Bible are about us. After all, when the apostle John writes in Revelation about the 144,000 standing around the throne of the Lamb, we are included in that number if we believe in Jesus. Those are not nameless symbols standing before the throne; they are the Christians of every land and every time whose voices ascend to shout: "Salvation belongs to our God who sits on the throne, and to the Lamb!" (Revelation 7:10). We are among the 144,000 singing to the Lamb. We stand with Moses and Elijah, Peter and Paul, Ruth and Mary.

> Around the throne of God
> The saints above and we on earth now stand,
> And all God's children here
> And those above who sing at His right hand,
> Divided by the veil of death,
> See death's dark veil now torn away,
> And sing in common voice
> To Father, Son and Spirit endlessly. [11]

When we unite in worship, we experience a marvelous fellowship. Through faith in Jesus Christ, Christians have become one family, sharing the same Father who made us, the same Brother who gave Himself for us, and living by the power of the same Holy Spirit who brought us to life through the Gospel. It is wonderful to gather together and use the prayers, songs, and stories that have been in the family for generations. In this way we not only preserve our Christian heritage, we also affirm our delight in our identity as children of the heavenly Father, celebrating with those who have gone before us in the faith and with those who are still to come.

CONCLUSION

LORD, IN YOUR MERCY— HEAR OUR PRAYER

Lord, in Your mercy—hear our prayer.
Work now a new creation,
As Word and water grant Your heir
The gifts of Your salvation.
Throughout his (her) life afford Your care;
And in the end grant him (her) a share
Of everlasting glory.

Lord Jesus, as You stood one day
Within the Jordan River,
Baptized by John to take away
Your people's sins forever,
Hear now Your people as they pray:

Forgive this child his (her) sins this day
And give to him (her) Your kingdom.

O Holy Spirit, grant Your grace
That faith in Christ may flourish.
Your Word is truth and in this place
Your Word our faith shall nourish.
Your Word gives life to water poured
Upon the heads, O gracious Lord,
Of all Your baptized people.

O Mighty Holy Trinity,
God, Father, Son and Spirit.
Your grace has set Your people free
Through Jesus' blood and merit.
Now free from sin and death and shame,
Absolved from every fault and blame,
We live to sing Your glory. Amen.[1]

*Christ the solid Rock remains always
at the heart of our confession
as Lutherans and as God's people.*

Why am I a Christian? Because Jesus is at the center
and it's all about Him. I am a Christian by grace, a simple yet
profound work of the new creation in water and Word. I
know Jesus loves me because "[His] Word gives life to water
poured." Because of Jesus, I face no punishment for sin, nor

do I face an eternal death. I am God's child, and He has given me His family of believers wherein He feeds me. God is so kind and gracious. Thus I live with faith in Him and hope that is born from His promises.

I am a Lutheran for the same reason I am a Christian. It is not by choice but by grace. The teachings of the Lutheran Church place Jesus at the center because the teachings of the Scriptures place Jesus at the center. No other confession demonstrates such fidelity to the truths of God's Word. No other confession so glorifies Christ by placing Him at the center of all it confesses and teaches. Being a Lutheran is truly all about Jesus.

- The entire sinful world is loved by Jesus.
- God saves us through the life, suffering, death, and resurrection of Jesus.
- The Holy Spirit creates faith by showing us Jesus.
- In Baptism, we die and rise with Jesus.
- In the Lord's Supper, we receive our inheritance with the body and blood of Jesus.
- The pastor proclaims and distributes the merits of Jesus.
- All our prayers go to the Father through Jesus.
- All our good works flow out of hearts that trust in Jesus.
- In the bearing of all crosses in this veil of tears, our eyes are fixed on Jesus.
- We wait with joyous hope for the day when we will see the face of Jesus.

Thus the Christian faith is all about Jesus. Being a Lutheran is all about Jesus. St. Paul says, "No one can lay a foundation other than that which is laid, which is Jesus Christ" (1 Corinthians 3:11). St. Peter says, "There is salvation in no one else, for there is no other name under heaven given among men by which we must be saved" (Acts 4:12). That's why we sing: "On Christ, the solid rock, I stand; All other ground is sinking sand."[2] Christ the solid Rock remains always at the heart of our confession as Lutherans and as God's people. The mission of the church becomes clear when it flows from Jesus and His work. Faith is living and grows where it is confessed because Jesus enables it to live and grow. We lift high the cross because on that cross is Jesus, the Savior, the hope of the entire world. Him we proclaim until everyone throughout the world praises Him with us.

People throughout the world need Jesus, which returns us to the Great Commission. Mission work is near the heart of every Christian and every Christian church. Throughout this book, I've used Matthew 28:19ff. to speak about God's Word, Jesus' work, Baptism, the Lord's Supper, and the life of the church. We do not fully grasp the Christian faith if we don't realize how it leads to proclamation and missions.

Once Christians experience the comfort of knowing their sins have been paid for completely by Jesus, how can we not want our family and friends to know the same comfort? Our Lord calls each of us in our Baptism to proclaim this comforting message. Mothers will want to ensure their children are baptized. Fathers will want to raise their families in this faith because of the comfort of forgiveness in Jesus. Families will seek opportunities at work or in school to bring this comforting message to others, inviting friends, other family members, and neighbors to church to hear and learn the Gospel.

Spirituality and faith frequently are used as modern moneymakers, but the world is lost when it makes spirituality and faith something humans must discover and work out on their own. The Christian church is called to inform the world of true spirituality in the means of grace. The body of Christ will proclaim this comforting message—that the true God has done all the work for our salvation—to a spiritually starved world. The Christian church gives the world someone to believe in—Jesus Christ.

The missionary zeal of St. Matthew's Gospel finds its culmination in the Great Commission, which is a commission to the church, to pastors, and to all believers to let people know where Christ is found. For those in need, for those who sin, for those who suffer, Jesus has located Himself in His Word, in Baptism, and in the Lord's Supper. The missionary proclamation is not an empty and individualistic proclamation. It is a proclamation to those who need to belong to the communion of saints, the church. In the end, there is no mission work apart from the church, the body of believers. Our daily mission activity always returns to the font, the pulpit, and the altar to be forgiven and to be fed by Christ and His gifts.

Thus our prayer is also for the lost souls in the world. When we say "Hear our prayer," it is for the mission field before us. It echoes what Jesus taught to the eleven disciples in the last chapter of Matthew. Disciples are made through the miracle of Gospel proclamation, which creates faith. Disciples are made through the cleansing waters of Baptism. Disciples are there when Christ fulfills His promise to forgive us and to be with us until the end of the age in the Feast of Victory of our Lord.

Christians want the world to know of this Christ who is at the center of Scriptures, of creation, of all life. In Jesus Christ God's creation finds purpose and hope. Christian missionary zeal is based on Christ and what He gives to the world. That hope for the whole world is why Christians and Christian churches will always be about missions.

Missions is why the church body in which I serve, The Lutheran Church—Missouri Synod, was formed. Constitutionally, our church body has three specific purposes: missions, the training of pastors and teachers, and the publication of the message of the Gospel. Why is mission work such a high priority? Certainly our Lord told us to go and make disciples, but we also are mission-minded because of the gifts Christ gives. Each of us has personally experienced and enjoyed the peace of Christ in the Gospel. This is the same message of forgiveness, comfort, hope, and salvation that has been the focus of this book. And everyone in the world needs that message, including us, our families, our friends, and our neighbors.

When Jesus is at the center, when everything is all about Jesus, there is no end. As a pastor, I did not dislike officiating at funerals. Instead of an ending, I knew this service to be a new beginning for every believer. This truth was never so clear to me as it was when my father passed away. Although he was a pastor, theologian, seminary president and professor, and author, most important to me, Robert Preus was my dad. My father's funeral was one of those moments that the Lord uses to show us what really counts, and I was intensely focused on every single aspect of this worship service. Despite my father's accomplishments, the numerous theologians and dignitaries and friends and family members in attendance, the funeral service, from beginning to end, was focused on Jesus Christ.

Our loved ones who die in the faith are alive.

Before the funeral began, I stared at the casket, which was draped in a funeral pall. The pall reminded me of Christ's holiness. My dad was a baptized child of God. My dad was alive because Jesus declared him to be holy by faith. Therefore, I knew my dad was raised out of the darkness of death into the light of Christ. What better way for a funeral to begin? What a powerful reminder that our baptized loved ones are children of God and wear the robes of Christ's righteousness. Our loved ones who die in the faith are alive.

The sermon text for the funeral was one of my dad's favorite Bible verses, a passage I had heard him preach on often: "This is a faithful saying, and worthy of all acceptation, that Christ Jesus came into the world to save sinners; of whom I am chief" (1 Timothy 1:15 KJV). The closing hymn included a prayer to Jesus that sums it all up for my dad, for me, and for every Christian:

> Thou hast died for my transgression,
> All my sins on Thee were laid;
> Thou hast won for me salvation,
> On the cross my debt was paid.
> From the grave I shall arise
> And shall meet Thee in the skies.
> Death itself is transitory;
> I shall lift my head in glory.[3]

From Baptism to death and through death into eternity, for every Christian—Jesus is at the center.

LUTHER'S SMALL CATECHISM

The Ten Commandments

As the head of the family should teach them in a simple way
to his household

The First Commandment

You shall have no other gods.

What does this mean? We should fear, love, and trust in God above all things.

The Second Commandment

You shall not misuse the name of the Lord your God.

What does this mean? We should fear and love God so that we do not curse, swear, use satanic arts, lie, or deceive by His name, but call upon it in every trouble, pray, praise, and give thanks.

The Third Commandment

Remember the Sabbath day by keeping it holy.

What does this mean? We should fear and love God so that we do not despise preaching and His Word, but hold it sacred and gladly hear and learn it.

The Fourth Commandment

Honor your father and your mother.

What does this mean? We should fear and love God so that we do not despise or anger our parents and other authorities, but honor them, serve and obey them, love and cherish them.

The Fifth Commandment

You shall not murder.

What does this mean? We should fear and love God so that we do not hurt or harm our neighbor in his body, but help and support him in every physical need.

The Sixth Commandment

You shall not commit adultery.

What does this mean? We should fear and love God so that we lead a sexually pure and decent life in what we say and do, and husband and wife love and honor each other.

The Seventh Commandment

You shall not steal.

What does this mean? We should fear and love God so that we do not take our neighbor's money or possessions, or get them in any dishonest way, but help him to improve and protect his possessions and income.

The Eighth Commandment

You shall not give false testimony against your neighbor.

What does this mean? We should fear and love God so that we do not tell lies about our neighbor, betray him, slander him, or hurt his reputation, but defend him, speak well of him, and explain everything in the kindest way.

The Ninth Commandment

You shall not covet your neighbor's house.

What does this mean? We should fear and love God so that we do not scheme to get our neighbor's inheritance or house, or get it in a way which only appears right, but help and be of service to him in keeping it.

The Tenth Commandment

You shall not covet your neighbor's wife, or his manservant or maidservant, his ox or donkey, or anything that belongs to your neighbor.

What does this mean? We should fear and love God so that we do not entice or force away our neighbor's wife, workers, or animals, or turn them against him, but urge them to stay and do their duty.

[The text of the commandments is from Ex. 20:3, 7, 8, 12–17]

The Close of the Commandments

What does God say about all these commandments? He says: "I, the Lord your God, am a jealous God, punishing the children for the sin of the fathers to the third and fourth generation of those who hate Me, but showing love to a thousand generations of those who love Me and keep My commandments." (Exodus 20:5–6)

What does this mean? God threatens to punish all who break these commandments. Therefore, we should fear His wrath and not do anything against them. But He promises grace and every blessing to all who keep these commandments. Therefore, we should also love and trust in Him and gladly do what He commands.

THE CREED

As the head of the family should teach it in a simple way
to his household

The First Article

CREATION

I believe in God, the Father Almighty, Maker of heaven and earth.

What does this mean? I believe that God has made me and all creatures; that He has given me my body and soul, eyes, ears, and all my members, my reason and all my senses, and still takes care of them.

He also gives me clothing and shoes, food and drink, house and home, wife and children, land, animals, and all I have. He richly and daily provides me with all that I need to support this body and life.

He defends me against all danger and guards and protects me from all evil.

All this He does only out of fatherly, divine goodness and mercy, without any merit or worthiness in me. For all this it is my duty to thank and praise, to serve and obey Him.

This is most certainly true.

The Second Article

REDEMPTION

And in Jesus Christ, His only Son, our Lord, who was conceived by the Holy Spirit, born of the Virgin Mary, suffered under Pontius Pilate, was crucified, died and was buried. He descended into hell. The third day He rose again from the dead. He ascended into heaven and sits at the right hand of God the Father Almighty. From thence He will come to judge the living and the dead.

What does this mean? I believe that Jesus Christ, true God, begotten of the Father from eternity, and also true man, born of the Virgin Mary, is my Lord,

who has redeemed me, a lost and condemned person, purchased and won me from all sins, from death, and from the power of the devil; not with gold or silver, but with His holy, precious blood and with His innocent suffering and death,

that I may be His own and live under Him in His kingdom, and serve Him in everlasting righteousness, innocence, and blessedness, just as He is risen from the dead, lives and reigns to all eternity.

This is most certainly true.

The Third Article

SANCTIFICATION

I believe in the Holy Spirit, the holy Christian church, the communion of saints, the forgiveness of sins, the resurrection of the body, and the life everlasting. Amen.

What does this mean? I believe that I cannot by my own reason or strength believe in Jesus Christ, my Lord, or come to Him; but the Holy Spirit has called me by the Gospel, enlightened me with His gifts, sanctified and kept me in the true faith.

In the same way He calls, gathers, enlightens, and sanctifies the whole Christian church on earth and keeps it with Jesus Christ in the one true faith.

In this Christian church He daily and richly forgives all my sins and the sins of all believers.

On the Last Day He will raise me and all the dead, and give eternal life to me and all believers in Christ.

This is most certainly true.

THE LORD'S PRAYER

As the head of the family should teach it in a simple way
to his household

Our Father, who art in heaven, hallowed be Thy name, Thy kingdom come, Thy will be done on earth as it is in heaven. Give us this day our daily bread; and forgive us our trespasses as we forgive those who trespass against us; and lead us not into temptation, but deliver us from evil. For Thine is the kingdom and the power and the glory forever and ever. Amen.

Our Father in heaven, hallowed by Your name, Your kingdom come, Your will be done on earth as in heaven. Give us today our daily bread. Forgive us our sins as we forgive those who sin against us. Lead us not into temptation, but deliver us from evil. For the kingdom, the power, and the glory are Yours now and forever. Amen.

The Introduction

Our Father who art in heaven.

Our Father in heaven.

What does this mean? With these words God tenderly invites us to believe that He is our true Father and that we are His true children, so that with all boldness and confidence we may ask Him as dear children ask their dear father.

The First Petition

Hallowed be Thy name.

Hallowed be Your name.

What does this mean? God's name is certainly holy in itself, but we pray in this petition that it may be kept holy among us also.

How is God's name kept holy? God's name is kept holy when the Word of God is taught in its truth and purity, and we, as the children of God, also lead holy lives according to it. Help us to do this, dear Father in heaven! But anyone who teaches or lives contrary to God's Word profanes the name of God among us. Protect us from this, heavenly Father!

The Second Petition

Thy kingdom come.

Your kingdom come.

What does this mean? The kingdom of God certainly comes by itself without our prayer, but we pray in this petition that it may come to us also.

How does God's kingdom come? God's kingdom comes when our heavenly Father gives us His Holy Spirit, so that by His grace we believe His holy Word and lead godly lives here in time and there in eternity.

The Third Petition

Thy will be done on earth as it is in heaven.

Your will be done on earth as in heaven.

What does this mean? The good and gracious will of God is done even without our prayer, but we pray in this petition that it may be done among us also.

How is God's will done? God's will is done

when He breaks and hinders every evil plan and purpose of the devil, the world, and our sinful nature, which do not want us to hallow God's name or let His kingdom come;

and when He strengthens and keeps us firm in His Word and faith until we die.

This is His good and gracious will.

The Fourth Petition

Give us this day our daily bread.

Give us today our daily bread.

What does this mean? God certainly gives daily bread to everyone without our prayers, even to all evil people, but we pray in this petition that God would lead us to realize this and to receive our daily bread with thanksgiving.

What is meant by daily bread? Daily bread includes everything that has to do with the support and needs of the body, such as food, drink, clothing, shoes, house, home, land, animals, money, goods, a devout husband or wife, devout children, devout workers, devout and faithful rulers, good government, good weather, peace, health, self-control, good reputation, good friends, faithful neighbors, and the like.

The Fifth Petition

And forgive us our trespasses as we forgive those who trespass against us.

Forgive us our sins as we forgive those who sin against us.

What does this mean? We pray in this petition that our Father in heaven would not look at our sins, or deny our prayer because of them. We are neither worthy of the things for which we pray, nor have we deserved them, but we ask that He would give them all to us by grace, for we daily sin much and surely deserve nothing but punishment. So we too will sincerely forgive and gladly do good to those who sin against us.

The Sixth Petition

And lead us not into temptation.

Lead us not into temptation.

What does this mean? God tempts no one. We pray in this petition that God would guard and keep us so that the devil, the world, and our sinful nature may not deceive us or mislead us into false belief, despair, and other great shame and vice. Although we are attacked by these things, we pray that we may finally overcome them and win the victory.

The Seventh Petition

But deliver us from evil.

But deliver us from evil.

What does this mean? We pray in this petition, in summary, that our Father in heaven would rescue us from every evil of body and soul, possessions and reputation, and finally, when our last hour comes, give us a blessed end, and graciously take us from this valley of sorrow to Himself in heaven.

The Conclusion

For Thine is the kingdom and the power and the glory forever and ever.* Amen.

For the kingdom, the power, and the glory are Yours now and forever. Amen.*

What does this mean? This means that I should be certain that these petitions are pleasing to our Father in heaven, and are heard by Him; for He Himself has commanded us to pray in this way and has promised to hear us. Amen, amen means "yes, yes, it shall be so."

*These words were not in Luther's Small Catechism.

THE SACRAMENT OF HOLY BAPTISM

As the head of the family should teach it in a simple way
to his household

First

What is Baptism?

Baptism is not just plain water, but it is the water included in God's command and combined with God's word.

Which is that word of God?

Christ our Lord says in the last chapter of Matthew: "Therefore go and make disciples of all nations, baptizing them in the name of the Father and the Son and of the Holy Spirit." [Matt. 28:19]

Second

What benefits does Baptism give?

It works forgiveness of sins, rescues from death and the devil, and gives eternal salvation to all who believe this, as the words and promises of God declare.

Which are these words and promises of God?

Christ our Lord says in the last chapter of Mark: "Whoever believes and is baptized will be saved, but whoever does not believe will be condemned." [Mark 16:16]

Third

How can water do such great things?

Certainly not just water, but the word of God in and with the water does these things, along with the faith which trusts this word of God in the water. For without God's word the water is plain water and no Baptism. But with the word of God it is a Baptism, that is, a life-giving water, rich in grace, and a washing of the new birth in the Holy Spirit, as St. Paul says in Titus chapter three:

"He saved us through the washing of rebirth and renewal by the Holy Spirit, whom He poured out on us generously through Jesus Christ our Savior, so that, having been justified by His grace, we might become heirs having the hope of eternal life. This is a trustworthy saying." [Titus 3:5-8]

Fourth

What does such baptizing with water indicate?

It indicates that the Old Adam in us should by daily contrition and repentance be drowned and die with all sins and evil desires, and that a new man should daily emerge and arise to live before God in righteousness and purity forever.

Where is this written?

St. Paul writes in Romans chapter six: "We were therefore buried with Him through baptism into death in order that, just as Christ was raised from the dead through the glory of the Father, we too may live a new life." [Rom. 6:4]

CONFESSION

How Christians should be taught to confess

What is Confession?

Confession has two parts.

First, that we confess our sins, and

second, that we receive absolution, that is, forgiveness, from the pastor as from God Himself, not doubting, but firmly believing that by it our sins are forgiven before God in heaven.

What sins should we confess?

Before God we should plead guilty of all sins, even those we are not aware of, as we do in the Lord's Prayer; but before the pastor we should confess only those sins which we know and feel in our hearts.

Which are these?

Consider your place in life according to the Ten Commandments: Are you a father, mother, son, daughter, husband, wife, or worker? Have you been disobedient, unfaithful, or lazy? Have you been hot-tempered, rude, or quarrelsome? Have you hurt someone by your words or deeds? Have you stolen, been negligent, wasted anything, or done any harm?

A Short Form of Confession

[Luther intended the following form to serve only as an example of private confession for Christians of his time. For a contemporary form of individual confession, see *Lutheran Worship*, pp. 310–11.]

The penitent says:

Dear confessor, I ask you please to hear my confession and to pronounce forgiveness in order to fulfill God's will.

I, a poor sinner, plead guilty before God of all sins. In particular I confess before you that as a servant, maid, etc., I, sad to say, serve my master unfaithfully, for in this and that I have not done what I was told to do. I have made him angry and caused him to curse. I have been negligent and allowed damage to be done. I have also been offensive in words and deeds. I have quarreled with my peers. I have grumbled about the lady of the house and cursed her. I am sorry for all of this and I ask for grace. I want to do better.

A master or lady of the house may say:

In particular I confess before you that I have not faithfully guided my children, servants, and wife to the glory of God. I have cursed. I have set a bad example by indecent words and deeds. I have hurt my neighbor and spoken evil of him. I have overcharged, sold inferior merchandise, and given less than was paid for.

[Let the penitent confess whatever else he has done against God's commandments and his own position.]

If, however, someone does not find himself burdened with these or greater sins, he should not trouble himself or search for or invent other sins, and thereby make confession a torture. Instead, he should mention one or two that he knows: In particular I confess that I have cursed; I have used improper words; I have neglected this or that, etc. Let that be enough.

But if you know of none at all (which hardly seems possible), then mention none in particular, but receive the forgiveness upon the general confession which you make to God before the confessor.

Then the confessor shall say:

God be merciful to you and strengthen your faith. Amen.

Furthermore:

Do you believe that my forgiveness is God's forgiveness?

Yes, dear confessor.

Then let him say:

Let it be done for you as you believe. And I, by the command of our Lord Jesus Christ, forgive you your sins in the name of the Father and of the Son and of the Holy Spirit. Amen. Go in peace.

A confessor will know additional passages with which to comfort and to strengthen the faith of those who have great burdens of conscience or are sorrowful and distressed.

This is intended only as a general form of confession.

What is the Office of the Keys?*

The Office of the Keys is that special authority which Christ has given to His church on earth to forgive the sins of repentant sinners, but to withhold forgiveness from the unrepentant as long as they do not repent.

Where is this written?*

This is what St. John the Evangelist writes in chapter twenty: The Lord Jesus breathed on His disciples and said, "Receive the Holy Spirit. If you forgive anyone his sins, they are forgiven; if you do not forgive them, they are not forgiven." [John 20:22–23]

What do you believe according to these words?*

I believe that when the called ministers of Christ deal with us by His divine command, in particular when they exclude openly unrepentant sinners from the Christian congregation and absolve those who repent of their sins and want to do better, this is just as valid and certain, even in heaven, as if Christ our dear Lord dealt with us Himself.

*This question may not have been composed by Luther himself but reflects his teaching and was included in editions of the catechism during his lifetime.

THE SACRAMENT OF THE ALTAR

As the head of the family should teach it in a simple way
to his household

What is the Sacrament of the Altar?

It is the true body and blood of our Lord Jesus Christ under the bread and wine, instituted by Christ Himself for us Christians to eat and to drink.

Where is this written?

The holy Evangelists Matthew, Mark, Luke, and St. Paul write:

Our Lord Jesus Christ, on the night when He was betrayed, took bread, and when He had given thanks, He broke it and gave it to the disciples and said: "Take, eat; this is My body, which is given for you. This do in remembrance of Me."

In the same way also He took the cup after supper, and when He had given thanks, He gave it to them, saying, "Drink of it, all of you; this cup is the new testament in My blood, which is shed for you for the forgiveness of sins. This do, as often as you drink it, in remembrance of Me."

What is the benefit of this eating and drinking?

These words, "Given and shed for you for the forgiveness of sins," show us that in the Sacrament forgiveness of sins, life, and salvation are given us through these words. For where there is forgiveness of sins, there is also life and salvation.

How can bodily eating and drinking do such great things?

Certainly not just eating and drinking do these things, but the words written here: "Given and shed for you for the forgiveness of sins." These words, along with the bodily eating and drinking, are the main thing in the Sacrament. Whoever believes these words has exactly what they say: "forgiveness of sins."

Who receives this sacrament worthily?

Fasting and bodily preparation are certainly fine outward training. But that person is truly worthy and well prepared who has faith in these words: "Given and shed for you for the forgiveness of sins."

But anyone who does not believe these words or doubts them is unworthy and unprepared, for the words "for you" require all hearts to believe.

DAILY PRAYERS

How the head of the family should teach his household
to pray morning and evening

Morning Prayer

In the morning when you get up, make the sign of the holy cross and say: In the name of the Father and of the Son and of the Holy Spirit. Amen.

Then, kneeling or standing, repeat the Creed and the Lord's Prayer. If you choose, you may also say this little prayer:

I thank You, my heavenly Father, through Jesus Christ, Your dear Son, that You have kept me this night from all harm and danger; and I pray that You would keep me this day also from sin and every evil, that all my doings and life may please You. For into Your hands I commend myself, my body and soul, and all things. Let Your holy angel be with me, that the evil foe may have no power over me. Amen.

Then go joyfully to your work, singing a hymn, like that of the Ten Commandments, or whatever your devotion may suggest.

Evening Prayer

In the evening when you go to bed, make the sign of the holy cross and say: In the name of the Father and of the Son and of the Holy Spirit. Amen.

Then kneeling or standing, repeat the Creed and the Lord's Prayer. If you choose, you may also say this little prayer:

I thank You, my heavenly Father, through Jesus Christ, Your dear Son, that You have graciously kept me this day; and I pray that You would forgive me all my sins where I have done wrong, and graciously keep me this night. For into Your hands, I commend myself, my body and soul, and all things. Let Your holy angel be with me, that the evil foe may have no power over me. Amen.

Then go to sleep at once and in good cheer.

How the head of the family should teach his household
to ask a blessing and return thanks.

Asking a Blessing

The children and the members of the household shall go the table reverently, fold their hands, and say:

The eyes of all look to You, [O Lord,] and You give them their food at the proper time. You open Your hand and satisfy the desires of every living thing (Psalm 145:15–16).

Then shall be said the Lord's Prayer and the following:

Lord God, heavenly Father, bless us and these Your gifts which we receive from Your bountiful goodness, through Jesus Christ, our Lord. Amen.

Returning Thanks

Also, after eating, they shall, in like manner, reverently and with folded hands say:

> Give thanks to the Lord, for He is good, His love endures forever. [He] gives food to every creature. He provides food for the cattle and for the young ravens when they call. His pleasure is not in the strength of the horse, nor His delight in the legs of a man; the Lord delights in those who fear Him, who put their hope in His unfailing love (Psalm 136:1, 25; 147:9–11).

Then shall be said the Lord's Prayer and the following:

> We thank You, Lord God, heavenly Father, for all Your benefits, through Jesus Christ, our Lord, who lives and reigns with You and the Holy Spirit forever and ever. Amen.

TABLE OF DUTIES

Certain passages of Scripture for various holy orders and positions, admonishing them about their duties and responsibilities

To Bishops, Pastors, and Preachers

The overseer must be above reproach, the husband of but one wife, temperate, self-controlled, respectable, hospitable, able to teach, not given to drunkenness, not violent but gentle, not quarrelsome, not a lover of money. He must manage his own family well and see that his children obey him with proper respect. 1 Tim. 3:2–4

He must not be a recent convert, or he may become conceited and fall under the same judgment as the devil. 1 Tim. 3:6

He must hold firmly to the trustworthy message as it has been taught, so that he can encourage others by sound doctrine and refute those who oppose it. Titus 1:9

What the Hearers Owe Their Pastors

The Lord has commanded that those who preach the gospel should receive their living from the gospel. 1 Cor. 9:14

Anyone who receives instruction in the Word must share all good things with his instructor. Do not be deceived: God cannot be mocked. A man reaps what he sows. Gal. 6:6–7

The elders who direct the affairs of the church well are worthy of double honor, especially those whose work is preaching and teaching. For the Scripture says, "Do not muzzle the ox while it is treading out the grain," and "The worker deserves his wages." 1 Tim. 5:17–18.

We ask you, brothers, to respect those who work hard among you, who are over you in the Lord and who admonish you. Hold them in the highest regard in love because of their work. Live in peace with each other. 1 Thess. 5:12–13

Obey your leaders and submit to their authority. They keep watch over you as men who must give an account. Obey them so that their work will be a joy, not a burden, for that would be of no advantage to you. Heb. 13:17

Of Civil Government

Everyone must submit himself to the governing authorities, for there is no authority except that which God has established. The authorities that exist have been established by God. Consequently, he who rebels against the authority is rebelling against what God has instituted, and those who do so will bring judgment on themselves. For rulers hold no terror for those who do right, but for those who do wrong. Do you want to be free from fear of the one in authority?

Then do what is right and he will commend you. For he is God's servant to do you good. But if you do wrong, be afraid, for he does not bear the sword for nothing. He is God's servant, an agent of wrath to bring punishment on the wrongdoer. Rom. 13:1–4

Of Citizens

Give to Caesar what is Caesar's, and to God what is God's. Matt. 22:21.

It is necessary to submit to the authorities, not only because of possible punishment but also because of conscience. This is also why you pay taxes, for the authorities are God's servants, who give their full time to governing. Give everyone what you owe him: If you owe taxes, pay taxes; if revenue, then revenue; if respect, then respect; if honor, then honor. Rom. 13:5–7

I urge, then, first of all, that requests, prayers, intercession and thanksgiving be made for everyone—for kings and all those in authority, that we may live peaceful and quiet lives in all godliness and holiness. This is good and pleases God our Savior. 1 Tim. 2:1–3

Remind the people to be subject to rules and authorities, to be obedient, to be ready to do whatever is good. Titus 3:1

Submit yourselves for the Lord's sake to every authority instituted among men: whether to the king, as the supreme authority, or to governors, who are sent by him to punish those who do wrong and to commend those who do right. 1 Peter 2:13–14

To Husbands

Husbands, in the same way be considerate as you live with your wives, and treat them with respect as the weaker partner and as heirs with you of the gracious gift of life, so that nothing will hinder your prayers. 1 Peter 3:7

Husbands, love your wives and do not be harsh with them. Col. 3:19

To Wives

Wives, submit to your husbands as to the Lord. Eph. 5:22

They were submissive to their own husbands, like Sarah, who obeyed Abraham and called him her master. You are her daughters if you do what is right and do not give way to fear. 1 Peter 3:5–6

To Parents

Fathers, do not exasperate your children; instead, bring them up in the training and instruction of the Lord. Eph. 6:4

To Children

Children, obey your parents in the Lord, for this is right. "Honor your father and your mother"—which is the first commandment with a promise—"that it may go well with you and that you may enjoy long life on the earth." Eph. 6:1–3

To Workers of All Kinds

Slaves, obey your earthly masters with respect and fear, and with sincerity of heart, just as you would obey Christ. Obey them not only to win their favor when their eye is on you, but like slaves of Christ, doing the will of God from your heart. Serve wholeheartedly, as if you were serving the Lord, not men, because you know that the Lord will reward everyone for whatever good he does, whether he is slave or free. Eph. 6:5–8

To Employers and Supervisors

Masters, treat your slaves in the same way. Do not threaten them, since you know that He who is both their Master and yours is in heaven, and there is no favoritism with Him. Eph. 6:9

To Youth

Young men, in the same way be submissive to those who are older. All of you, clothe yourselves with humility toward one another, because, "God opposes the proud but gives grace to the humble." Humble yourselves, therefore, under God's mighty hand, that He may lift you up in due time. 1 Peter 5:5–6

To Widows

The widow who is really in need and left all alone puts her hope in God and continues night and day to pray and to ask God for help. But the widow who lives for pleasure is dead even while she lives. 1 Tim. 5:5–6

To Everyone

The commandments . . . are summed up in this one rule: "Love your neighbor as yourself." Rom. 13:9

I urge . . . that requests, prayers, intercession and thanksgiving be made for everyone. 1 Tim. 2:1

> *Let each his lesson learn with care,*
> *And all the household well shall fare.*

NOTES

Introduction

1. *The Lutheran Hymnal* (St. Louis: Concordia, 1941), 85:1–3.

Chapter One

1. *Lutheran Worship* (St. Louis: Concordia, 1982), 517:3.

Chapter Two

1. Augsburg Confession II, 1–3, in *The Book of Concord*, ed. Theodore Tappert (Philadelphia: Fortress, 1959), 29.

2. The word *Calvary* is Latin for the Greek word that means "skull." The Greek word appears only once in the New Testament in Luke 23:33, which reads: "And when they came to the place that is called The Skull, there they crucified Him, and the criminals, one on His right and one on His left."

3. Jaroslav Pelikan, ed. and trans., *Lectures on Galatians 1535*, vol. 26 of Luther's Works (St. Louis: Concordia, 1963), 277–78, 280.

4. C. F. W. Walther, "Christi Auferstehung: Unser Sieg," trans. Daniel Preus (sermon presented Easter Sunday, 1846). Mark 16:1–8 apparently was one of Walther's favorite pericopes; he preached on this text sixteen times.

5. W. A. Lambert, trans., "The Freedom of a Christian," in *Career of the Reformer I*, ed. Harold J. Grimm, vol. 31 of Luther's Works, ed. Helmut Lehmann (Philadelphia: Fortress, 1957), 352.

6. Lowell J. Satre, trans., "Two Kinds of Righteousness," in *Career of the Reformer I*, ed. Harold J. Grimm, vol. 31 of Luther's Works, ed. Helmut Lehmann (Philadelphia: Fortress, 1957), 297, 298.

7. *Lutheran Worship* (St. Louis: Concordia, 1982), 362:1.

8. *Lutheran Worship*, 370:1–2.

9. *The Lutheran Hymnal* (St. Louis: Concordia, 1941), 380:1.

10. *The Lutheran Hymnal*, 380:5.

11. Walther, "Christi Auferstehung: Unser Sieg."

12. Walther, "Christi Auferstehung: Unser Sieg," (*emphasis added*).

13. From the explanation of the Third Article of the Apostles' Creed in *Luther's Small Catechism with Explanation* (St. Louis: Concordia, 1986), 15.

14. Smalcald Articles III, 12, 2, in *The Book of Concord*, ed. Theodore Tappert (Philadelphia: Fortress, 1959), 315.

15. Smalcald Articles III, 8, 3, in *Book of Concord*, 312.

16. Harold L. Senkbeil, *Sanctification: Christ in Action* (Milwaukee: Northwestern, 1989), 24. Senkbeil is quoting from George M. Marsden, *Fundamentalism and American Culture* (New York: Oxford University Press, 1980), 99f.

17. Martin Luther, *The Bondage of the Will*, trans. James I. Packer and O. R. Johnston (Tarrytown, N.Y.: Fleming H. Revell, 1957), 103–4.

18. Sydney E. Ahlstrom, *A Religious History of the American People* (New Haven: Yale University Press, 1972), 450.

19. Senkbeil, *Sanctification*, 25.

20. Charles G. Finney, *Lectures on Systematic Theology: Selections* (Minneapolis: Bethany Fellowship, 1979), 179.

21. Finney, *Lectures on Systematic Theology*, 46.

22. Finney, *Lectures on Systematic Theology*, 320, 322.

23. Finney, *Lectures on Systematic Theology*, 326.

24. Finney, *Lectures on Systematic Theology*, 326–27.

25. C. F. W. Walther, *The Proper Distinction between Law and Gospel*, trans. W. H. T. Dau (St. Louis: Concordia, 1929), 268.

26. Walther, *Proper Distinction between Law and Gospel*, 269 (*Walther's emphasis*).

27. From the explanation of the Second Article of the Apostles' Creed in *Luther's Small Catechism*, 14.

28. *Evangelical Lutheran Hymnary* (St. Louis: MorningStar Music Publishers, 1996), 517:2.

Chapter Three

1. See Gene Edward Veith Jr., *The Spirituality of the Cross* (St. Louis: Concordia, 1999).

2. See "Section III: Table of Duties," in *Luther's Small Catechism*, annotated by Edward W. A. Koehler (Fort Wayne, Ind.: Concordia Theological Seminary Press, 1981), 16–19.

3. Formula of Concord, Solid Declaration, IV, 10–12, in *The Book of Concord*, ed. Theodore Tappert (Philadelphia: Fortress, 1959), 552–53.

Chapter Four

1. Martin H. Bertram, trans., *Sermons on the Gospel of St. John: Chapters 14–16*, vol. 24 of Luther's Works, ed. Jaroslav Pelikan (St. Louis: Concordia, 1961), 7.

2. Apology of the Augsburg Confession XII, 158 60, in *The Book of Concord*, ed. Theodore Tappert (Philadelphia: Fortress, 1959), 207.

3. Bertram, *Sermons on the Gospel of St. John*, 193–94.

4. *Lutheran Worship* (St. Louis: Concordia, 1982), 295:1–3.

5. *The Lutheran Hymnary* (Minneapolis: Augsburg, 1935), 81:1.

Chapter Five

1. From the explanation of the Sacrament of Holy Baptism in *Luther's Small Catechism with Explanation* (St. Louis: Concordia, 1986), 22.

2. From the explanation of the Sacrament of the Altar in *Luther's Small Catechism with Explanation* (St. Louis: Concordia, 1986), 29.

3. This view would be a distorted "interpretation" of Jesus words in John 1:17: "For the law was given through Moses; grace and truth came through Jesus Christ."

4. *Lutheran Worship* (St. Louis: Concordia 1982), p. 166.

5. See "What is the benefit of this eating and drinking?" in the explanation of the Sacrament of the Altar in *Luther's Small Catechism*, 29.

6. From the explanation of the Sacrament of the Altar in *Luther's Small Catechism*, 29.

7. *Lutheran Worship*, p. 148.

Chapter Seven

1. *The Lutheran Hymnal* (St. Louis: Concordia, 1941), 167:1–2a.
2. *The Lutheran Hymnal*, 207:2.
3. *Lutheran Worship* (St. Louis: Concordia, 1982), 464:3–4.

Chapter Eight

1. Augsburg Confession V, 1–3, in *The Book of Concord*, ed. Theodore Tappert (Philadelphia: Fortress, 1959), 31.
2. Charles M. Jacobs, trans., "A Sermon on Keeping Children in School," in *The Christian in Society III*, ed. Robert C. Schultz, vol. 46 of Luther's Works, ed. Helmut Lehmann (Philadelphia: Fortress, 1967), 219–20.
3. John W. Doberstein, ed. and trans., "Sermon on Soberness and Moderation," in *Sermons I*, vol. 51 of Luther's Works, ed. Helmut Lehmann (Philadelphia: Fortress, 1959), 299.
4. Martin H. Bertram, trans., "Sermons on the First Epistle of St. Peter," in *The Catholic Epistles*, vol. 30 of Luther's Works, ed. Jaroslav Pelikan (St. Louis: Concordia, 1967), 134.
5. Carl W. Folkemer, trans., "Explanations of the Ninety-five Theses," in *Career of the Reformer I*, ed. Harold J. Grimm, vol. 31 of Luther's Works, ed. Helmut Lehmann (Philadelphia: Fortress, 1957), 231.
6. Folkemer, "Explanations of the Ninety-five Theses," 209.
7. C. F. W. Walther, *The Proper Distinction between Law and Gospel*, trans. W. H. T. Dau (St. Louis: Concordia, 1929), 236–37.
8. Walther, *Proper Distinction between Law and Gospel*, 361.

Chapter Nine

1. Carl S. Meyer, ed., *Moving Frontiers* (St. Louis: Concordia, 1964), 149.
2. Meyer, *Moving Frontiers*, 150.
3. Meyer, *Moving Frontiers*, 150.
4. Meyer, *Moving Frontiers*, 151.
5. *Lutheran Worship* (St. Louis: Concordia, 1982), p. 136.
6. *Lutheran Worship*, p. 137.
7. *Lutheran Worship*, p. 137.
8. *Lutheran Worship*, p. 137.
9. *Lutheran Worship*, 289:4 (*emphasis added*).
10. *Lutheran Worship*, pp. 147–48.
11. Jon Vieker and Daniel Preus, "Around the Throne They Stand" (St. Louis: Concordia, 2002), stanza 5.

Conclusion

1. Original text by Daniel Preus (May 2002).
2. *Lutheran Worship* (St. Louis: Concordia, 1982), 368 (refrain).
3. *The Lutheran Hymnal* (St. Louis: Concordia, 1941), 207:4.

The first thing expressed in my seal is a cross, black, within the red heart,

to put me in mind that faith in Christ crucified saves us.

Now although the cross in black, shameful,

and intended to cause pain,

yet it does not change the color of the heart,

does not destroy nature.

But this heart is fixed on the center of a white rose,

to show that faith causes joy,

comfort and peace.